MW01290203

A WAVE OF THE BATON

Doreen A. Betts

Copyright © 2011 by Doreen A. Betts

A Wave of the Baton
by Doreen A. Betts

Printed in the United States of America

ISBN 9781613792520

All rights reserved solely by the author. The author guarantees all contents are original and do not infringe upon the legal rights of any other person or work. No part of this book may be reproduced in any form without the permission of the author. The views expressed in this book are not necessarily those of the publisher.

Unless otherwise indicated, Bible quotations are taken from The New International Version of the Bible. Copyright © 1984 by Zondervan Publishing House.

www.xulonpress.com

Sharen,

Enjoy your time
with the Maestro!

Karen

DEDICATION

This book is dedicated to Joseph Hayes Smith, who has been the light of my life in recent years. His life is a miracle that I describe within the pages of this book.

You are a special person, Joseph, and God has a wonderful plan for your life. He has something for you to do that no one else can do, and He will totally prepare you for His purpose. I pray you seek the face and voice of God every day and recognize His Hand when it is upon you.

I love you Joseph with all my heart and I pray this book will cause you to draw near to the heart of God, your Creator, through your salvation which comes only from your acceptance of Jesus Christ as your personal Savior and Lord.

ACKNOWLEDGMENTS

There are many people who deserve to be acknowledged for their friendship, help, encouragement, and prayers they have offered. The list includes hundreds of family and friends who have been there for me for a reason, a season, or a lifetime.

I am especially grateful to Annie Wagner who shared her vision with me, and to Glenda Hogg and Dr. Jeri Hargrave who encouraged me in this endeavor.

I would also like to express my heartfelt gratitude to Kelly Scharosch, Karen Whittaker, and Warren Whittaker, and who agreed to serve as proofreaders and did a wonderful job. This is a tedious process and I thank you all from the bottom of my heart.

Forward

God speaks to us in many ways. In regard to writing this book, He spoke to me through inspiration, confirmation and encouragement.

While ironing one morning God spoke to my spirit and said, "You should write a book." Later that same morning, I was approached by a Godly woman who shared with me that while she was praying that day, God told her I was going to write a book.

He planted the inspiration in me and at the same time He was speaking to me, He spoke to her with the same message. She received it so strongly, she couldn't wait to tell me, and when she did, I knew it was confirmation from God that I should, indeed, write a book.

The seed was planted and I began to formulate it in my mind. I planned a week long trip to study and begin writing. Three days before I was to leave on my trip, my pastor's wife approached me and said, "You need to be writing." She had no idea of my plan to write a book, but she had read a short piece I wrote, and felt impressed to share her feelings with me. She has a doctorate degree, is a physician's assistant, as well as a professor of nursing at the university. Needless to say, I respect her intellect and her words served as added confirmation and encouragement.

God works in mysterious ways, often through other people. In my case, He worked in an orderly fashion—He first planted the inspiration in my heart and then He spoke through two other people I respect and trust to bring the inspiration, confirmation, and encouragement I needed to write this book.

All the glory, praise, and honor belongs to Him, and Him alone.

TABLE OF CONTENTS

Part One: Preparation...21

Part Two Revelation: The Blessings...137

Setting the Stage

One by one the musicians appear from the side doors, each impeccably dressed in black suits and white shirts or blouses. Quietly they make their way to their respective place in the orchestra pit. Each carefully examines their instrument which has been polished to a mirror finish and tuned to perfection. One by one they come, until the last and every seat is filled.

Each section of the orchestra is now complete; the strings, woodwinds, brass, percussion, and keyboards. For the orchestra to accomplish the precise sound that the composer intended, thus bringing the written score to life, each and every musician must be in their proper place and know their part. Whether a large part, or one single note, they are each responsible for their part. With every instrument at the ready, and the musicians practiced and prepared, they eagerly await what is soon to come.

Quietly through the side door, the Maestro appears. He is tall and straight, wearing a beautiful black silk tuxedo with tails, and a snow white shirt, adorned with a perfectly balanced black bow tie. His shoes are so highly shined they would pass the test of the strictest Inspector General. Not a hair on his head is out of place.

Under his arm he carries the score, holding it close to his body as to protect it from any danger, well aware of the treasure that lies within. He has studied it long and hard and knows every line of every passage. He has rehearsed to perfection the dynamics and cueing of each measure and movement. Without saying a word he fixes his eyes on the platform in the center of the pit, and moves slowly and gracefully toward it, almost as if he is floating. As he steps onto the platform, all conversation comes to a halt, and every eye moves in his direction.

Once on the platform, he steps to the podium and carefully puts the masterpiece in its place. Taking a deep breath, he takes a long hard look at the musicians, ensuring everyone is in their place, poised with their instruments. He begins by making eye contact with the person seated in the first chair of each section, beginning with the strings. First, the violins, moving to the violas, and on to the cellos, double bass, harp, and finally the guitar. His eyes move to the woodwind section which includes the piccolos, flutes, oboes, clarinets, bassoons, and the saxophones. He moves now to the brass section where his eyes meet those holding the trumpets, cornets, french horns, trombones, and tubas. Moving to the back of the pit he views the percussion section. The timpani, snare drum, bass drum, cymbals, triangle, tambourine, xylophone, glockenspiel, and chimes are at the ready. Finally, he makes eye contact with the musicians seated at the piano and the organ.

Having completed his perusal of every component of the orchestra, the anticipation mounts as the Maestro gently opens the score and smoothes the pages, revealing only to himself, page one. Once again he quickly looks over his musicians as they have now moved to the edge of their chairs. All is quiet. You can hear a pin drop as he makes his move. He reaches to the podium and picks up the baton with his right hand.

All eyes are on the Maestro as he slowly raises the baton. The awaited sound is heard. "Tap, tap, tap." With three taps of the baton, all instruments are raised to their playing position.

Finally, after one last glance around the pit, with the baton in his right hand, he raises both arms, and after a slight pause, he brings the baton down, creating the first down beat of the first measure. The overture has begun!

The piece moves fluidly like water running down stream; slowly at times, while raging over rushing rapids at others, as the score dictates. The tempo continuously changes as the various segments and passages come into play and the Maestro cues each dynamic with a mere stroke of the baton.

The quiet, peaceful trill of the piccolo smoothly slides into the romantic love song of the string section. The flutes sing their light, happy tune, and just as you think all is calm, he makes his move to the middle of the pit toward the brass, and a storm of horns can be heard in the distance as they approach with the growing crescendo demanded by the arm movements of the Maestro. Now the storm intensifies as he gives the cue adding the other horns and the timpani drums.

The Maestro's hands fly to the rhythm of the rage, his hair is now far from its original place, and his whole body is involved in the movement as he thrashes violently back and forth, until suddenly the dissonance begins to calm and this passage comes to an end. The storm has passed, now replaced by the beautiful, clear tone of the first chair violinist whose solo fills the room like the song of a single snow bird in the stillness of the cold winter air.

As the score moves from segment to segment, so does the story. Listening closely, you hear the percussionist maintaining the consistent beat, or heart beat, of the piece from the beginning to end. Also recognizable is the recurring theme, or passage, throughout the entire score. It may be a familiar melody line, a particular rhythm pattern, or a cavatina performed as a solo or by a group of musicians.

This musical phrase, or pattern, that seems to appear and reappear, brings a sense of solidarity to the whole score, creating a theme for the musical story, and is often referred to as the middle ground. It's that consistent part that makes for a soft place to land, and yet is firm enough to allow the next segment to spring forth.

Overtures range from short to rather long in length and have a variety of passages or segments that will eventually bring the piece to a close. Some will go out with the trumpets blaring and the final crash of the cymbals, while some just abruptly, and unexpectedly, end. Others, however, simply drift away with the lone, fading note of the oboe, like your best friend walking away into the sunset. As you stand watching, they finally disappear over the horizon, never to be seen or heard again.

Nevertheless, every overture comes to an end in some way, and at that time with a wave of the baton, the Maestro conducts the final beat of the final measure of the final passage. With that he places the baton down on the podium, closes the score, and takes a bow. It's over. His work here is completed.

Philippians 1:6 *"He who began a good work in you will carry it on to completion until the day of Christ Jesus."*

Introduction

Every human life is played out like an overture. God is the Composer, the Orchestrator, and the Maestro, who personally conducts every life overture in His magnificent creation. Everything about each of us is in our original score, which was written by Him. He has been at the podium conducting your life overture since the day you were born and He will be there until it comes to an end.

Through the different stages and times of your life, He has been right there, with the baton in His hand, cueing the additions and deletions of the people who serve as the musicians causing your life overture to play out according to the score He has written for you.

Never question the Composer, the Orchestrator, or the Maestro. He has never made a mistake and He never will. Every beat, measure, and passage of your life overture is exactly as He composed and orchestrated it, and is flawlessly conducting it. He knows every minute dynamic of the original score which has been written specifically for you.

Your score was written long before you were born. It is a single part of the master plan of the universe created by Almighty God.

Psalm 139:16 *"Your eyes saw my unformed body, all the days ordained for me were written in your book before one of them came to be."*

PART ONE

Preparation

The First Down Beat

On October 21, 1950 the great Maestro stepped onto the platform, approached the podium, picked up the baton, tapped it three times, and with the first down beat, my life overture began. Not with the crash of the cymbals, or with the sound of trumpets blaring, but in a timid way, perhaps with the low undertones of the cello section.

I grew up during the 1950's and 1960's in East Oakland, California, in a lower, middle class neighborhood, but by the time I got to Jr. High School, it had deteriorated considerably. What had been a fairly nice area in the 1950's, quickly became a ghetto by the mid-1960's. Life was not an easy or smooth melody, but more like staccato notes of several instruments each playing a different tune at the same time, which on rare occasion, would come into sync with each other.

To put it mildly, my mother was *not* an involved parent. My dad was the love of her life, and she was not concerned, or supportive, of a child's whim. The song they played together was a wonderful love song that did not include me. I was to be seen and not heard. I was not to speak unless I was spoken to. I learned quickly to obey my mother, doing exactly what I was told to do. The song of praise was seldom played, while the lament after the reprimand was heard often.

My mother led the percussion section producing an ever present rumble of fear in the background. It continuously overshadowed anything that remotely resembled the smooth, tranquility of joy or love from the string section or woodwinds.

My dad's calm, gentle hands played the only melody of love in my life overture. He played a wonderful song of security, hope, and contentment that I was allowed to snuggle up next to when my mother was busy in the kitchen. He and I had that special relationship that is often found between father and daughter, and I hoped he would be that safe place to fall should I ever need it.

The childhood passage of my life overture was one of mixed melodies and confused messages. The quiet song of my dad was discernable only when my mother briefly backed off on the drums, which was not often.

I longed to hear the sweet song of my dad, but the deafening pounding of my mother's drum made it very hard, if not impossible.

2 Corinthians 7:5 *"Conflicts on the outside, fears within."*

A New Musician

The Maestro however, was about to give the cue, and move my overture into a new segment. The song of a musician whose tone was often in a minor key, but whose rhythm was steady and strong, was about to be added.

Hers was the song with a wild, vivid imagination like that of the jazz saxophonist whose variations on the melody were so rampant and far removed, it was at times, impossible to catch the tune at all. A song of mystery and suspense that carried fun, lighthearted undertones, and brought joy and excitement to a little girl's heart.

Her melody was completely off the wall, out of touch with the norm, and off-key much of the time, but the steady beat in the background was the basis of her being. She was about to receive the cue to play her first part in my life overture, a part that would become a refrain to be played over, and over again for many years to come.

The steady beat that was her heart beat would be instilled in me and the strength of her song would give me a firm place to stand, and influence my life overture like no other. Her heart beat would become mine.

Just as the rumble of my mothers drums were becoming deafening, the Maestro gave the cue for this new addition, the song of my grandmother.

Psalm 40:2-3 *"...He set my feet on a rock and gave me a firm place to stand. He put a new song in my mouth...."*

Grandma

Grandma

I spent a lot of time with my unmarried grandmother, who was a very hard worker. She lost her home and everything she had in 1930 during the depression, and lived alone in a tiny, eight foot trailer house on a very meager income. She spent every weekend at our house, arriving Friday, and leaving Sunday.

Grandma was different. She didn't trust people, and she didn't like anyone except me. She lived in a world of make believe, made up stories. One could say she marched to the beat of a different drum. She never had much, but she always had time for me, and that's just what I needed. Together we played a fun, lighthearted, happy duet. I loved it when Grandma was there. She would cook me anything I wanted to eat for dinner, sometimes nothing but a big cast iron skillet full of fried onions. Other times it would be her world famous meat balls or meat loaf. Whatever it was, it was good.

Occasionally, during the summer months I would go home with her. Her tiny trailer was like our own little clubhouse. Together we sat on the top bunk and played rummy. We kept score for months at a time. I think she just kept the score going until I won. Sometimes that took a long time, but she wanted me to win.

Since she never learned to drive, she walked every where she went and/or took the bus. I loved spending time with her, and we had a lot of fun together. She taught me to work hard, and her song of encouragement was one I could count on. I can remember her saying time and time again, "Nothing takes the place of hard work. Lazy people don't get anywhere in this world." She was a survivor who wasn't afraid to get her hands dirty or blistered, and she sang the song of inspiration to a little girl who needed all the inspiration and encouragement she could get.

She loved to work outside in the yard, and one day while we were working in the flower garden, the Maestro gave her the cue to instill in me a work ethic that would serve me well throughout my life. I was about five years old, and we were sitting on the ground in the flower garden. She was pulling weeds and I sat next to her digging holes with a small trowel. All of a sudden she set her trowel down, looked me straight in the eye and said, "Kid, you have got to be the hardest working person I have ever seen in my life."

I'm sure she had no idea the importance of what she had said, but that day her words set the tone for my life overture, a melody that would become a recurring refrain.

Proverbs 14:23 *"All hard work brings a profit, mere talk leads only to poverty"*.

God Loves You

Talk of any subjects that remotely resembled anything spiritual was not to be heard at our house. Christmas was about presents, Santa Claus and snowmen, and Easter brought the Easter Bunny, egg hunts, foil wrapped chocolate rabbits, and yellow marshmallow chickens. However these holiday times did lend opportunity for the joyful song of the lighthearted flutes and piccolos which were very rarely able to be heard over the constant rumble of the timpani drum and the barking staccato of the trumpeting of my mother's voice.

My dad was a musician and played music with a country/western band every Friday and Saturday night. Since they wanted to sleep in on Saturday and Sunday mornings, when I was a very young child, my mother began to send me to Sunday School on the church bus. I knew early on that sending me to Sunday School on the bus was her way of getting rid of me, but at the same time, it was an opportunity to go somewhere, and I was happy to go anywhere where I might hear a different melody.

This was my first exposure to God. I liked Sunday School very much, especially the music. Certain hymns quickly became my favorites and would ring out in my mind throughout the week. I found solitude in being alone with those simple melodies that spoke so profoundly to me. Even as an adult these songs remained my favorites and I have relied on them to bring me back from that dark, lonely place I periodically found myself.

As a very small child, I can remember walking to the corner alone, where the church bus would stop, and pick me up. It was always on time, and the bus driver seemed happy to see me and would have kind words to say, unlike what I heard at home. Every Sunday morning I would wake up with a happy song in my heart knowing that the bus would take me to a place where the people were nice, and seemed to care about me. But why? I had no idea why, but they did. I knew there was something right about those people at church. The sweet message of the people there never changed: "God loves you," and they seemed to love me too.

Who was this God, and why would He love me? I was just a little kid who rode the bus, but the song in my heart was different there. For the first time in my life I could hear the beautiful love song of the string section. It was the love song of God.

Mark 10:14 " *...Let the little children come to me, and do not hinder them, for the kingdom of God belongs to such as these.*"

Let's Make Some Music!

My dad had a rather large family, and each Thanksgiving Day and Christmas Eve there was a gathering at his parent's home. All my aunts, uncles, and cousins would be there. It was great fun and something I looked forward to all year. Each member of the family played their part in the quick, joyful melody of fun and games each time we gathered together. That is, except for my mother, who being the anti-social person that she was, hated every minute of it and remained in the back of the pit rumbling on her drum. She went along only because my dad loved it so much. Consequently, I steered clear of her all day not wanting to hear her familiar drone of unhappiness and sour notes.

In the afternoon, all the kids played ball in the front yard, while the grown-ups did who knows what in the house. I had no idea what was going on in there. It was so crowded in that little house I didn't even try to go inside until after dinner. That's when the good part happened; what I had been waiting for all year.

It started by my Grandpa picking up his fiddle in one hand, his bow in the other, and announcing with excitement, "Alright, let's make some music!" Oh boy, let the fun begin! I was the first one in the house now. It didn't matter where my mother was; I was determined to make my way to the front room where they were going to make some music! My dad stood up his big bass fiddle, Uncle Vic lined up his harmonicas on top of the piano, and Aunt Emma took her place at the piano.

Boy could they make music, and it went on half the night! It was country music with a hint of blue grass thrown in, and I loved every minute. It was loud and every toe in the house was tapping in perfect time, including mine.

I don't remember how old I was when Aunt Emma first let me sit next to her on the piano bench while she "tickled the ivories," but once I had that place no one could take it from me. It didn't matter to me that my feet both quickly became numb from hanging in mid-air for hours. I would have endured anything to sit next to her and watch her hands as they moved effortlessly over the keys. She made it look so easy and I could see the pleasure she received from playing. Aunt Emma was a widow, but music brought her joy. I wanted to feel that; I wanted to play just like Aunt Emma.

Between this and the songs at church, my love for music was born. There was such a contrast between the two music types, but I loved it all, and with it the Maestro introduced a new dimension to my life's overture. From then on, no matter how bad things got, music became my safe place to land.

Ephesians 5:19 "...*Sing and make music from your heart to the Lord.*"

Piano Lessons

Being the artist and musician my dad was, I knew it was he I should ask about taking piano lessons. Finally after months of begging, my parents agreed. By no means were they about to purchase a piano, but they would consider renting one. This would be a big expense for our family, so I was determined to do the very best I could, knowing I would be playing just like Aunt Emma in no time.

The cost of a half hour lesson was twenty-five cents, and I would have to earn the money myself. After all, they were willing to rent the piano. There wasn't much work for a seven year old little girl in the city. How was I going to make twenty-five cents every week? Finally, it hit me; I could mow our lawn with our old push lawn mower. I liked being outside, and my mother hated doing it, so it seemed like the perfect job for me. My mother agreed and then told me I would have to have three months of lesson money saved up before they would rent a piano. Every Saturday I pushed the mower up and down the block, knocking on doors asking the lady of the house if I could mow her lawn. I got quite a few regular mowing jobs and I did the very best job I could. I even swept off their concrete walk as a bonus. I learned early on that if you go the extra mile, and do a little extra work, the chances are good you won't get fired or replaced. By the end of the summer I had three months of lesson money saved up, and my parents rented a piano.

Every Tuesday after school, I walked two blocks to Mrs. Ramsey's house for my lesson. It wasn't exactly what I had hoped it would be. Aunt Emma made it look so easy since she played by ear and was full of natural talent. I, on the other hand had no natural ability at all, and would have to learn everything.

Mrs. Ramsey was a mean old biddy who would hit the top of my hands with the metal edge of a ruler if they were not in the right position. She taught me piano theory and the basics. I quickly learned to read music and could play a few little songs, but what I learned the fastest was to keep my hands in the proper position to avoid bloody, black and blue knuckles. I had no natural ability, but I had the want to, and I was determined to play. At times I could see my dad cringe when I played a wrong note, but I persisted. I had my heart set on playing the piano, and the song of determination could be heard over the noise of the wrong keys I was playing.

As always, the song of encouragement came from my Grandma, "You just keep on practicing kid, you'll be good some day." I wasn't sure I believed her, but I loved to hear her say it.

James 5:11 *"As you know, we consider blessed those who have persevered..."*

Doreen at the piano

An Exciting Adventure

Grandma had four older sisters, two of whom played important roles in my life. During the summer Grandma's sister, Alice, would buy her a Greyhound bus ticket from Oakland, California to Gold Beach, Oregon where she lived. Grandma would spend two weeks working in her sister's flower beds. She enjoyed the trip, but the tune I played was one of sadness while she was away.

It was just before school was out, the summer I was eight years old, when Grandma asked me if I would like to go with her to Oregon for two weeks to visit Aunt Alice. I couldn't believe my ears. I was getting to go somewhere; me, the kid. I was really excited until it hit me. Would my mother let me go? Probably not, she didn't let me do anything.

As it turned out, Grandma had already discussed it with my mother and Aunt Alice was buying the ticket. It was a done deal, I was going on a real adventure as soon as school was out, and I couldn't wait. As the last day of school approached, all I could hear was a jubilant song of excitement complete with clanging cymbals, which intensified daily as our departure date drew closer.

What a trip this was going to be for a little girl who had never been out of Alameda County much less the state of California. Grandma was as excited as I was, and our duet of anticipation rang out as we prepared for the adventure which was ahead.

The Maestro had picked up the tempo of my life overture and it was running wild. The strings were racing, the horns were all ablaze with excitement, and the beat of the percussion section was so fast the drum sticks were a blur. I had never been more excited about anything in my life.

I didn't know it, but the Maestro was about to introduce a new musician into my life overture that played instruments I had never seen, and melodies and rhythms I had never heard. A musician that would bring a whole new dimension to my life and show me things I never knew even existed.

Numbers 16:30 *"...the Lord will bring about something totally new..."*

Aunt Alice

Aunt Alice was really fun. Like my grandmother, she didn't have a husband. Her husband had died a few years earlier, and she was quite capable of taking care of herself. She was the first person I ever saw reading their Bible. She faithfully read it every morning before getting out of bed. While I was at her house, I would lie beside her in her bed and she would read the Bible to me. I knew there was something right about that.

Aunt Alice was different than anyone I had ever met in my life. First of all, she was very wealthy. I really didn't know we were poor until I met Aunt Alice. She lived ten miles up the Rogue River from Gold Beach, Oregon, in a huge home that was once a fishing lodge. Her late husband loved to fish, and when they retired they bought the lodge so he could fish with his buddies.

Her home was filled with priceless antiques and she was a ham radio operator. Every day she would sign on by speaking into the big microphone, saying, "This is W7DVH, Alice here. Can you hear me? This is W7DVH, Alice here." Out of a giant piece of equipment that took up half the room, with hundreds of knobs and dials, came a voice in response to hers. It was one of her friends from somewhere across the sea. She had friends all over the world, and they communicated via ham radios.

You can imagine the excitement I felt as an eight year old little girl being a part of such an event. She would introduce me to whomever it was she was talking to and then allow me to talk to them. "Push the button to talk, and release the button to listen." were her instructions. What fun! These people were somewhere half way around the world and I was actually talking to them. Unbelievable!

Aunt Alice had the gift of hospitality. She was always having people over to her house for dinner or going some place to play cards or to a lodge meeting. She loved people and loved having fun. Sometimes she would dress up in funny clothes and make a surprise visit to a friend. She knew everyone and everyone knew her. She was the first person I knew who was social, and I wanted to be just like her.

Grandma and I went to Aunt Alice's house every summer for four years. I learned a lot from Aunt Alice, as the Maestro conducted her welcoming song of hospitality accompanied by her roaring laughter as it echoed through her huge home and the chambers of my heart.

Romans 12:13 *"Share with Gods people who are in need. Practice hospitality."*

Aunt Alice

Aunt Lil

Aunt Lil was Grandma's oldest sister, and she too was a widow. Like oldest girls in any family, she was the boss. She was a take charge person and when Aunt Lil spoke, everyone listened, except Grandma of course, who wasn't going to let anyone tell her what to do.

Aunt Lil was a domestic goddess. She was an excellent seamstress and a very good cook. As she lived relatively close to us, I spent quite a bit of time at Aunt Lil's while she sewed clothes for me. She was very good at making something beautiful out of a bag of rags. She was always sewing something; a quilt, an apron, a dress for herself or someone else. I can remember standing on her kitchen table for what seemed like hours as she pinned the hem in the dress she was making for me. Her house was immaculate and she was meticulous about her work. "Everything has a place, and everything needs to be in its place." she would say.

She operated in her kitchen just as she did in her sewing room. She never threw anything away if she could use it to make something else. What she did throw away she fed to her chickens in the back yard. She grew a very nice, small garden every year and had several fruit trees. She canned the fruit and vegetables which she stored in her basement for the winter.

Aunt Lil liked to keep up with world affairs. She had a radio in her sewing room and faithfully listened to Walter Winchell every day. "It's important to know what's going on in this old world. We need to be informed so we can stay one step ahead of them." I never knew who them was, and I never asked her what she meant because my mother taught to be quiet and listen, not ask questions.

Unlike Aunt Alice, Aunt Lil wasn't what you would call fun. She was prim and proper and very active in her community. She went to church every Sunday, and belonged to several lodges. She believed in being committed to everything she was involved in. I can recall her telling me many times, "If you are going to belong to something, take part, don't just sit back and let someone else do all the work."

Aunt Lil played a large part in my life overture. The constant hum of her treadle sewing machine and the buzz of busyness was a perfect compliment to the counterpoint rhythm of commitment to her family, church, and community. Her song made for some reassuring, smooth background music in my life, which the Maestro knew I desperately needed.

Proverbs 31:27 *"She watches over the affairs of her household and does not eat the bread of idleness."*

Aunt Lil

Work With All Your Might

When I was eleven years old, my Grandma bought a piece of land in the mountains with a lump sum of money she received from Social Security. It was the first property she owned since 1930. This land would offer me the opportunity to learn more than I could ever imagine.

It was two acres covered with trees and brush. There was no water, no electricity, nothing, except a lot of work. My grandmother, who was 62 years old at the time, could visualize what it would look like some day when she and I were finished with it. She had long ago shared with me her melody of work, and it was about to become a harmonious duet we would play together.

She and I spent every summer vacation (all three months of it) at the property working to clear it and make it beautiful. My parents would drop us off the day after school was out, and pick us up the day before school started in the fall.

We slept in sleeping bags on the ground in a tent, and cooked our meals over an open fire. I loved every minute of it. Together we could do whatever we set our minds to. The lyrics to our work song were, "We can do it, we just have to learn how." I missed our summer trips to Aunt Alice's house in Oregon, but this was an exciting new adventure with the opportunity to really accomplish something.

That first summer, the Maestro gave the cue for a new tune in my life overture. I played the saw, and we both played the hammer and nails, as we tackled the first of many building projects that would be in my future. Grandma and I built a six foot by eight foot shed. It was a bit out of square, but it was built well, didn't leak and was still standing in 2003 when the property was sold.

Grandma didn't drive, so every day we walked down the dusty hill to town and pulled back our red wagon which carried a five gallon aluminum thermos full of ice. By the time we got back, we had the water we needed for that day.

Over the next few summers we accomplished a lot on the property. In the years to come she had a well drilled and electricity brought in, which made our stay much easier but not nearly as much fun.

The familiar melody of work, productivity, and accomplishment was becoming the theme song of my life overture. No matter what the situation, I was ready, willing, and able to roll up my sleeves, dig in my heels, and do whatever it took to get the job done.

Ecclesiastes 9:10 *"Whatever your hands find to do, do it with all your might..."*

Junior High School

J unior High School brought a huge adjustment to my life. The two blocks I was used to walking to school, would now be over two miles through neighborhoods that had deteriorated dramatically. I was always rather athletic, and this increased greatly when I started running to and from school as fast I could. I was a small kid and I wasn't going to take any chances on the bad kids catching me, so I ran both ways with everything I had.

Junior High School brought with it more than fear. The Maestro had someone very special to add to my life overture, and she received her cue on the first day of school. I was scared to death, and when I took my seat in my homeroom class, a little girl, even smaller than I, came and sat down in the chair right next to me. Her name was Karen Riddervold and we immediately struck up a friendship that would last a lifetime. From that day forward Karen and I have played a duet in perfect harmony. From the first day we blended together like twin sister violinists, as our song of friendship began.

Karen offered me far more than friendship when she invited me to join an organization she belonged to called the International Order of Job's Daughters. I had heard of it because my cousin belonged, but I never dreamed I would ever have the opportunity to be involved in something so special. Karen encouraged me to talk to my parents about joining, but I was hesitant. She didn't know my parents.

If I wanted to be involved in something, I would have to make it happen myself. I can recall my mother barking at me over and over again like the quick, back and forth bow movements on the low strings of the viola, "I don't care if you do it, but don't ask me for any money, don't ask me for a ride, don't ask me for anything. Figure it out for yourself." Over the years I learned to figure things out for myself, and this time was no different. I went straight to Aunt Lil. She would be the one to convince my mother it would be good for me, and I was right. Aunt Lil was thrilled that I had made friends with a girl in Job's Daughters, and she would talk to my mother.

It took a year for Aunt Lil to finally convince my mother that I should be able to join. She assured her that she would sew any dresses I needed, etc. With that, Aunt Lil moved to first chair violinist in my orchestra. She had just accomplished the impossible, and in mid November, 1963, the Maestro gave the cue to a whole new section of musicians, as I was initiated into Bethel No. 195 of the International Order of Job's Daughters, in Oakland, California.

Proverbs 18:24 *"...there is a friend who sticks closer than a brother."*

Job's Daughters

My new musicians were the caring, devoted girls and adults who were involved in Job's Daughters. The two that played the most caring song I had ever heard in my life were Karen's parents, Mr. and Mrs. Olav Riddervold. I had never met people like them. They offered me the opportunity to be active in the Bethel as they went out of their way to come and pick me up and take me home for every meeting and function. They made sure I had a ride anywhere I wanted to go. Until I met them, I didn't know what parents should be like. Now, I knew.

I took very seriously my various positions and duties in Job's Daughters. It was a place of belonging for me; something I could be a part of; a family. Based on the book of Job in the Bible, it offered additional Christian teachings to what I had been taught at Sunday School and Children's Church. The teachings were good and noble, and I considered myself fortunate to be a part of such an honorable organization. I worked hard and did the very best I could at every office I held and every committee I served on. I also vowed to myself, that if I should ever have children, I would be a parent like the many parents who reached out and helped me at this time in my life when I needed it so badly.

My years spent in Job's Daughters were the highlight of my early life, and its many songs rang out loud and strong in my life overture. During this passage, every instrument was in perfect harmony with the rest. The love song of the string section was blended perfectly with the joy and happiness of the flutes and piccolos, while the deep, underlying tones of the cellos and double bass spoke to structure, order, and self discipline. All the while the drums kept the steadfast, consistent beat by which I was taught so many good life lessons. I'm certain I learned more about being a productive member of society and general life application of Biblical principles than I would have learned in my entire life without it. I will always be grateful to my closest, dearest, and life-long friend Karen, and to her parents who never chose to leave me behind.

The book of Job teaches that if through the trials and tribulations of life, we remain steadfast and faithful to God, and exercise patience in all situations, we will receive our honored reward. The song we sung to close every meeting as we knelt on the floor in a cross formation, was *Nearer My God to Thee*. This song would become a refrain to be played over, and over again in my life overture, as I did my best to draw nearer to God.

Job 42:15 *"Nowhere in all the land were there found women as beautiful as Job's daughters, and their father granted them an inheritance..."*

Improvising

All the while I continued to take piano lessons. After a year of renting a piano, my parents saw that I was serious about playing and actually bought a piano for $50.00. Mrs. Ramsey had moved away and the Maestro was about to cue another musician who could play the piano even better than Aunt Emma. Aunt Lil had a friend who gave piano lessons and arranged for her to teach me.

This transition in teachers took place while I was in Jr. High School, and I had to take the bus from school and then walk about 1/2 mile to her house. Her name was Mrs. Etta Halsey. She was old, and played the piano for several lodges and even at Carnegie Hall once. She was good! In speaking with her on the phone she told me to bring whatever music I had been playing with me to my first lesson. I shall never forget that first lesson.

Her house was a cluttered mess with stacks of music piled all over the piano. Her first question was, "Let's see what you've been playing?" I handed her my red, John Thompson book. She looked at me over the top of her glasses and said, "Is this what you WANT to play?" I had never been asked what I wanted to play; I had only been told what I was going to play. My response was simply a shrug of my shoulders. "How 'bout you play something you would like to play? Do you listen to the radio?" Of course I listened to the radio, what thirteen year-old girl didn't? "Do you know where the music store is on MacArthur Blvd.? Here, take this lesson money back and go to the music store and buy something you want to learn to play, and we'll go from there next week."

I left her house with a whole new outlook on piano lessons. I had learned all the basics from Mrs. Ramsey, but now Mrs. Halsey was going to make it fun! I went straight to the music store and bought a copy of *Ramblin' Rose* by Nat King Cole. On the way home I wondered what my mother was going to say, or if she would even believe my story. When I got home, I told my parents what Mrs. Halsey said and showed them what I chose to play. I will never forget my dad's response as he took the piece of sheet music from me, "Now you're talking, this is something we can play together."

Together? We were going to play together? Oh boy, my dream of playing like Aunt Emma just might be coming true. I had practiced long and hard on all that dull, boring music, but now things were going to be different, I just knew it. That day I was singing a new song, the song of hope; hope to some day make music with my dad.

1 Samuel 16:17 *"...Find someone who plays well and bring him to me."*

My Lifelong Friend

Over the next three years the piano took on a whole new meaning to me. Mrs. Halsey allowed me to play anything I wanted along with some pieces she wanted me to play as well. It wasn't easy, but for the first time the challenge was fun. She taught me to play chords and to improvise. She was an expert at making a piece come alive and making it her own. This was a completely foreign concept to me as Mrs. Ramsey taught me to play exactly what was on the written page with no deviation whatsoever. "We are to play what is written; what the composer wrote." Mrs. Halsey, on the other hand said, "Feel the music; play it the way you feel it; improvise on it; make it your own. That's when it will become fun." It took some time, but eventually I began to get it.

The drudgery of practice was replaced by pleasure, and the piano was no longer just a musical instrument, but a companion and therapist. It became my soft place to fall when I felt alone or hurt; my best friend who I could always count on to bring a smile to my face no matter what. Together we made great music.

During this time there came an opening as Musician (the piano player) in Job's Daughters. This was my big chance, and I jumped at it. Mrs. Halsey's face lit up like a Christmas tree when I told her I had accepted the office at the piano. Also, with her encouragement, I played with the instrumental orchestra for two years in Jr. High School. All of this lent to versatility in my playing. I learned that there are times to play what's on the written page, and times to play to suit yourself. With that my life overture took on a lilt of improvisation.

On Thanksgiving Day, 1964, my dad told me to bring my music along to my grandparent's home. I was so nervous that afternoon, I couldn't eat, but when Grandpa announced we were going to make some music, I took Aunt Emma's place on the piano bench and she sat next to me. With my Dad on bass, my Uncle Vic on harmonica, and my Grandpa on fiddle, together we played Ramblin' Rose, country/western/bluegrass style. We played it several times, and after starting off slow as it was written, my dad said, "Let's pick it up." We picked it up alright. That was the swingingest version of Ramblin' Rose anyone ever heard, and one of the highlights of my musical life. That night I became a part of a musical picture I had watched my whole life. Aunt Emma hugged me so tight I thought she was going to break my ribs.

When the Maestro gave the cue for the piano to begin in my life overture, and sat me on the bench, He knew I would need a life long friend who would never forsake me. The piano would be that friend, and together we would play away the sad times and rejoice in the good.

1 Samuel 16:16 *"...play when an evil spirit...comes upon you and you will feel better."*

High School

The Maestro had some new fast and furious music to introduce that would represent my high school years. It consisted primarily of a fast paced bass drum; boom, bo-bo-boom, bo-bo-boom; a beat to run by, and run fast.

My neighborhood had deteriorated to the point that I was unable to attend the high school near our house for fear of being killed. Again Aunt Lil stepped in. She had a friend that lived in San Leandro who would allow me to use her address and go to Pacific High School. Once again, I would have to make it happen myself, which meant leaving the house at 5:00 AM and walk (or I should say, run) six blocks, in the dark, to East 14th Street where I would catch the bus to school in San Leandro. This was scary at times as the people in the area didn't take kindly to little white girls in their neighborhood. For three years I did this in order to go to school and get my high school diploma. It was hard, but the Maestro stood ready to wave the baton once again.

I never made any real friends in high school for fear the Principal would find out I was going to school out of my district, and throw me out. I did well at school and enjoyed sports and of course, music. They didn't need a piano player in the orchestra so I took choir instead. I was shocked and thrilled, when I was asked to sing the second soprano part in the eight member a cappella ensemble, called the "Pacific Singers." I also had a part in all the musical plays.

My vocal music teacher's name was Mr. Bond, and he was great! He taught me a lot about vocal music and encouraged me to sing every chance I got. Under his strict direction I learned to hear harmony, and sing parts. He had a great sense of humor, but demanded excellence in our music and expected our voices to blend perfectly together. I worked very hard to do my part to achieve that perfect balance he was listening for. Our group was invited to sing at various community events as well as all the school functions. I was proud to be chosen as one of the eight.

Mr. Bond was the best school teacher I ever had. He was a wise man and taught me far more than music. His voice was bigger than life, like that of the entire brass section, each playing their part to perfection. He brought light to my world of darkness. As I ran to the bus stop each morning, my thoughts would turn to my music class and the big smile I knew would be on Mr. Bond's face. With a song in my heart, the fear of the people possibly lurking in the shadows seemed to fade, and I ran even faster.

Hebrews 12:1 *"...let us throw off everything that hinders...and let us run with perseverance the race marked out for us."*

Moving On

I didn't take hard classes in high school, I took classes that interested me and ones that would help me find a job upon graduation. College was out of the question, as there was certainly no money for that.

In addition to my music and required classes, I took business classes; bookkeeping, typing and office machines. They came easy for me and I achieved straight "A's" with no problem. I graduated 4.0, at the top of my class, which caused the familiar tune of accomplishment to once again be heard loudly as a part of my overture. This time the Maestro conducted *Pomp and Circumstance* as I proudly walked across the stage and shook hands with the Principal as he presented me my diploma. I had done it, and school for me, was over.

Being the independent person I was, and desperately wanting to earn some money, I immediately went in search of work. Being a very fast typist, I easily got a job with a nationwide insurance company. As always, I was a hard worker, and was promoted quickly and often. With each promotion came a pay increase and the sound of money in the bank sang the sweet song of independence to my ears.

I knew if I was going to be totally independent I would have to own a car, so I saved every dime I could. The one good lesson I learned from my mother was not to be in debt, and so I saved. As soon as I saved enough, I paid cash for my first car. I also had the money for insurance and some set aside for repairs as well.

Life was good. I was making my own way except for one thing; I was still living at home. I knew I didn't make enough money to rent an apartment, so my options were slim to none.

The Maestro would soon wave the baton and cue a male musician to take part in my overture. He was tall and handsome, four years older than I, lived on his own, drove a sports car, and had a job. Was this the string section playing the love song I had dreamed of for so long? I was nineteen years old and positive I recognized the song when I heard it. Shortly after, Gary and I were married.

All I could hear was the love song of the strings which I allowed to drown out any other melody. It was the sweet melody that accompanies the love between a man and a woman, and the freedom that came with it.

Song of Solomon 1:4 *"Take me away with you—let us hurry..."*

Michelle

It wasn't long before I could detect some off-key sounds amid the love song. The flat notes and melody imperfections became more and more prevalent. I knew I had made a big mistake, but my song of determination was strong and I was not about to give up.

I worked hard to make our marriage a success, but the harder I worked, the less Gary worked. Then I had an idea: maybe if we had a baby it would bring life to our relationship and a sense of responsibility to Gary. Three years into our marriage the Maestro introduced a new song into my life overture; the sweet cry of a baby girl. Michelle.

My plan to bring joy, happiness and a sense of responsibility to Gary did not materialize, and our relationship quickly went down-hill like a sliding trombone. Gary was not the man he originally portrayed himself to be. He was lazy, couldn't hold a job, and had gotten us in debt up to our ears.

My responsibilities, on the other hand, had increased considerably. I was working a full time job at the insurance company, taking care of a baby, doing the housework and yard work, while he sat on the couch watching television, eating cookies, and collecting unemployment.

We had turned the page on the duet we once played together, and now we were not even playing in the same key. I was playing my theme song of work with all my heart, while his only contribution was the monotonous sound of his snoring as he lay asleep on the back row. This song would have to come to an end…..soon!

Shortly after Michelle's first birthday, I got my ducks in a row, rented an apartment near a girlfriend, and moved out. Our marriage song was over. I knew I could make it on my own. After all, I had been playing this song as a solo for a long time while dragging him behind like a tuba tied to my leg.

My song of work continued but now it was somehow easier and lighter. The low pitched, heaviness of the trombone that seemed to be forever lagging behind a full measure, was no longer there. It wasn't an easy song to play, but it had a lilt of hope; hope of a future.

My mother kept Michelle for me while I was at work, and every evening after picking her up I would sing my favorite hymns to her in the car as we drove home to our little apartment. The songs from my childhood days at Sunday School and Job's Daughters were my lifeline. The message of comfort and strength found in the lyrics is what held me together as a single parent.

Psalm 41:9 *"Even my close friend, whom I trusted...has lifted up his heel against me."*

The Love of My Life

On November 12, 1973 the Maestro gave the cue to a man who would play a part in my life overture like no other. What would seem like a by-chance meeting to most, would prove to be exactly how the composer wrote it, and orchestrated it. On that day, exactly on cue, I met the love of my life, Jack Betts.

He was nine years older than I, and was a well established salesman for a large wholesale lumber company. I was immediately attracted to him, but was not about to quickly jump into his song for another ride on a slide trombone, if you know what I mean. I did however agree to give him my phone number, and he called the very next day.

For our first date he asked me if I would like to get up early the following Sunday and go for a ride to the Sacramento area, which was about 100 miles away. He wanted to go see his mother and take her to church. I had not been in church for several years, as my church had been sold to a Black Muslim congregation shortly after I was saved and baptized, but I agreed to go if we could take Michelle along, who was then 16 months old.

That Sunday, Jack picked Michelle and me up, and off we went for a long ride to somewhere called Wilton, California which was close to Sacramento. On the trip Jack talked and I listened. I had become familiar with the song of liars, and I knew in my heart Jack was playing a melody that was pure and true. He shared with me a life truth he had been taught by his mother and always lived by: "I am no better than anyone else, and no one is better than I am."

Jack had come from meager beginnings in Oklahoma and moved to California with his family in 1950. He worked from the time he was four years old selling something and/or building something. Hard work was the story of his whole life; hard work, honesty, integrity, generosity, and faith in God. That's what Jack Betts was all about.

He was playing my tune, and as I listened I could hear my own song playing right along with his, as we stood on the same middle ground.

Psalm 15: 2-5 *"He whose walk is blameless and who does what is righteous, who speaks the truth from his heart and has no slander on his tongue, who does his neighbor no wrong and casts no slur on his fellowman, who despises a vile man but honors those who fear the Lord, who keeps his oath even when it hurts, who lends his money without usury and does not accept a bribe against the innocent. He who does these things will never be shaken."*

Jack

Ruby

U pon meeting Jack's mother, Ruby Betts, the Maestro cued one of the most powerful musicians to take part in my life overture. Ruby played the most consistent melody of faith I would ever hear. They were long sustained whole notes of pure, true, total commitment to God. No matter how long she held the note, it never wavered.

Jack's mother was a wonderful person and she accepted me, and my daughter Michelle, immediately. She was a widow and was self sufficient, living every day of her life by faith in God. I had never met anyone like her before. She never worried about anything or anyone, she simply trusted God to take care of the situation and her, which He did.

Ruby worked hard her whole life. She raised five children in Oklahoma where life was far from easy. For two years during WWII they lived in California where Ruby worked as a welder along side her husband and other men.

Ruby always found something good or positive to say about people, no matter who they were or what they were doing. A cup with a single drop in the bottom was almost full to Ruby, and the most off-key, out of tune song was a sweet melody to her ears. She was a calm person and never got too excited about anything. "Worry" was a word that was not in her vocabulary.

She read and studied her Bible every day with a fervor that was new to me. She faithfully went to church every Sunday, taught Sunday School, and participated in any and all activities of her church.

Ruby was a rock, a solid rock of faith and obedience that set an example for me I had never seen before. Her song never changed and neither did she. She had the patience of Job, and would give you her last dollar if she thought you needed it, knowing it would come back to her ten fold, which it always did.

I listened as she effortlessly played her theme song of faith day after day, every day without fail. I wanted to play along with her, but it was a song I had never heard before and very hard to play. I watched and listened as the melody flowed out of her like an accomplished harpist whose hands create beautiful, angelic music. Perhaps some day I would catch on to her tune.

Proverbs 3:5 *"Trust in the Lord with all your heart, and lean not on your own understanding;"*

Ruby

Life on the Ranch

Jack was a people person with hundreds of friends and a huge family. Everyone loved Jack, and it wasn't long before that list included me. Once again I heard the string section playing the song of love in my heart. Although this time it wasn't just the string section, it was the whole orchestra in absolute harmony, blended together perfectly creating pure balance. It was the same balance my high school music teacher, Mr. Bond, longed to achieve in our voices. I knew in the depth of my being the Maestro had waved the baton and cued the man of my dreams. Together we could make beautiful music as our life overtures joined.

After Jack and I were married, we moved to the country in Wilton, California. Being a city girl, I knew nothing about country life. I had never seen a cow, a horse, or a snake, or anything else you see on a ranch. Fortunately I adapted to it nicely (except the snakes) and within two weeks I was milking a cow twice a day. We had a big garden and grew many of our own vegetables. I loved everything about my new life.

Jack and Ruby knew about life on the ranch, and I was eager to learn all I could. They taught me to grow a garden, can food, make butter, doctor cows, butcher steers, build fences, and drive the tractor. It was hard work, but after all that was my song and I played it well!

There was an old house on the property and Jack and I totally remodeled it. This was my first experience with serious building and I jumped into it with both feet. My love for building came to life during this project, and the song that accompanied it came naturally for me. The house turned out great! It wasn't long before we were building another one from the ground up, and then another.

Life was good on the ranch; a lot to learn and a lot to do. My life overture had taken on a few new instruments like cow bells, milk buckets, and tractor engines. I quickly learned to play them all well. My theme song of work could once again be heard loud and strong. The song of productivity, diligence, and accomplishment was the perfect complimentary piece.

It was that same tune my Grandma played for me in her minor keys so many years ago, but now I was playing it myself in a major key, and it felt right.

Proverbs 13:4 *"...the desires of the diligent are fully satisfied."*

The Beat Goes On

In the first three years of our marriage, Jack and I remodeled one house, built two others from the ground up, and constructed a large barn. I learned a lot from Jack about building and how structures are put together. I liked being on the job and learning as much I could about everything possible.

My knowledge of lumber and building materials had begun to expand, but I had a lot to learn which I was eager to do. I would often recall my Grandma singing the familiar lyrics, "You can do it Kid, you just have to learn how."

Late in 1977, Jack and I started our own wholesale lumber business. After taking Michelle to school, I went to work at the lumber yard. In addition to keeping the books and managing the office, I learned to dispatch trucks and do some sales. I even learned to drive the forklift. What the heck, if I could drive the tractor at home, surely I could drive a forklift, right? Right; and I did. Later, I learned to drive the trucks as well. If there was something to learn, I was eager to learn it.

Again, it was the words my Grandma spoke to me at an early age that encouraged me, "You are the hardest working person I have ever seen." Those words became my byline, and were the perfect lyrics and driving force for my song of productivity, self-confidence, and accomplishment.

Hardly a day went by that I didn't hear my Grandma's song in my head, and it was always positive and upbeat. She never said anything negative to me, and it was her confidence in me that instilled the "want to" I have had my whole life.

Her words became the heart beat of my life overture; steadfast, strong, consistent, and even. That's what a heart beat should be, and Grandma sat in the percussion section of my orchestra where she maintained that strong, steady tempo until she died at the age of 92.

Psalm 112:7 *"...his heart is steadfast, trusting in the Lord."*

Family Life

Our overtures were playing the same song in the same key as we worked side by side together. Whatever the job, together we could do it. Jack had more experience and knowledge than I, and his song was like that of a confident french horn setting the goals for our life together.

After watching my Aunt Lil for so many years, I had picked up her ability to make something out of nothing, and to figure out how to make things work. Consequently I played the song of ingenuity pretty well, which was a compliment to any song played on the ranch.

I was bound and determined to be a good parent, and to use all the knowledge I had to teach Michelle everything I could. Under no circumstances would I play the same tune to her my mother played to me. I did my best to sing to her the song of opportunity and encouragement, and support her in her interests, while allowing her to fall when she needed to. These were the times when the sorrowful sound of the double bass could be heard moaning in the background as her slightest setback or poor decision, ripped at my heart strings.

Michelle was an easy child and had a love for animals. She enjoyed her dog and riding her horse on the ranch. She and Jack used their horses to pen cattle, occasionally entering a competition where they always did well. For the most part she played a happy childhood tune which brought joy to my life.

Michelle belonged to Job's Daughters in Elk Grove, California and I did my best to support her and fulfill the vow I made myself so many years ago...my promise to do what I could to help any girl whose parent was not interested, involved, or able. This time of giving on my part brought many blessings back to me in the form of true thankfulness from the girls I was able to help.

It was a busy, happy time in our lives with all the activities, and the rewards were many. Once again I had the opportunity to sit at the piano and play when the Bethel was without a Musician. Twenty years later, the songs were the same. Among them, *Holy Holy Holy, Sweet Hour of Prayer, Come Holy Spirit, Onward Christian Soldiers, and Nearer My God to Thee.* It made for a sweet refrain, one that reminded me of the many good lessons I learned so long ago, and the hope that Michelle was learning them as well.

Proverbs 20:11 *"Even a child is known by his actions, by whether his conduct is pure and right."*

Michelle

Only By Faith

Our song was not always smooth. We suffered our share of disappointments and setbacks, but the Maestro knew exactly how to modulate our song from one key to the next, eventually bringing us back into sync where things sounded right. Whatever discord could be heard was overridden by the ever present refrain of determination Jack and I played so well together.

Included always were the true, clear notes of honesty and integrity with absolutely no variations in those tones. A handshake was as strong as any signed, legal, binding contract, and your word was a commitment to stand by no matter what. Consequently, the perfect pitch of good character blended in precise harmony with the middle ground theme of work we both played.

After listening to Ruby's song of faith for several years, I was beginning to catch on to the melody. Jack had learned this song as a child, but it was one that took some time for me. Eventually, it was our faith in God that was the chord that held us together in the bad and sad times.

We both believed in the goodness of God and trusted in His promise to never leave us or forsake us. Many times this was all we had, but we knew it was all we needed. It was during these times when the Maestro would cue the orchestra to play one of my old favorite hymns, and I found myself sitting on the piano bench allowing my dear friend to bring peace to my soul and hope to my broken heart.

As the years passed our twin overtures were playing a complex melody. The determination of the snare drum, the integrity of the finely tuned cello, the honest tones of the oboe, and the persistence of the entire percussion section, all played the background music for the spiritual sounds of the magnificent pipe organ. This made for a beautiful composition that lasted for many years and eventually resulted in success.

Midway through this passage of our overture, the Maestro inserted an interlude. It was an old familiar song to Jack that he loved, but had not heard for a long, long time. I had never heard it before, but it was one that I would soon come to love as well.

Psalm 119: 1-2 *"Blessed are they whose ways are blameless, who walk according to the law of the Lord. Blessed are they who keep His statutes and seek Him with all their heart."*

Back Home

In the summer of 1982 we attended a family reunion in Atoka, Oklahoma. I had known for years that Jack was from Oklahoma, and I had heard many stories about "back home," but on this trip all the stories came to life as I met so many of the people I had heard about for so long.

Jack talked the most about Ward's Chapel, and I discovered on that trip that it was a community out in the country, seven miles west of Atoka. While we were there, Jack again relived the stories of his childhood, and the endurance and fortitude of the Betts family and his Choctaw heritage.

What seemed like a storybook setting was a real place and had not changed much since 1950, when Jack's family moved to California. He told story after story as we drove the country roads of the community, recalling which of his aunts or uncles lived on each corner. We spent a long time walking the property where he was born, known as Grandma Betts' place. The house had burned down, but we sat together on the ground where it once stood. Jack picked up a handful of soil, rubbed it together in his hands, and let it run slowly through his fingers. I watched as he traveled back in time in his mind; back to a time he loved so much. He had so many vivid memories of the life and times in the Ward's Chapel community during the 1940's.

At the Ward's Chapel cemetery, we found many gravesites of his ancestors who had put their hearts and souls into this community and the little church they loved so much. The church was founded by his great-great grandparents, before Oklahoma was even a state, when it was still Indian Territory. He told how they went to church in a wagon pulled by a team of horses. It didn't matter how bad the roads were, they didn't miss church at Ward's Chapel.

That day I saw Jack's demeanor change. He took on a sense of belonging; of roots in a community; his roots. I had never seen Jack happier. He was home and we both knew it.

This interlude was played by Jack alone as a solo. Over the years he had played so many instruments in my overture but now he picked up a different one. It was one he used to play, but had sat in the corner for a long, long time. These refound memories brought back the longing to play it once again, and with a wave of the baton, the Maestro brought Jack's old song back to life.

Hebrews 13:7 *"Remember your leaders who spoke the word of God to you. Consider the outcome of their way of life and imitate their faith."*

His Old Friend

Our trip to Oklahoma made a difference in Jack, and one evening after work, he slowly and quietly got out of his chair and made his way to the corner of our living room where it stood in the corner. He gently picked it up, took his handkerchief out of his pocket and dusted it off. Going outside he took a seat on the porch with his long time friend. I followed but never uttered a word, and keeping my distance, I watched and listened as Jack renewed his friendship with his long lost friend.

Touching each string one at a time, he quickly had it tuned, and for the first time in a long, long time, he brought life to his guitar. A bit rusty at first, but it wasn't long before he and his old friend were playing like they used to.

Every night after work he would sit with his old friend on his knee and play. He remembered all the old cowboy songs his dad sang to him as a child back home, but each night he would end with his favorite. It was impossible for him to play it without tears coming to his eyes. He longed for his home so much, and each time he played it, I longed for it too. The song was *Oklahoma Hills*. This simple, old cowboy melody, expressed Jack's feelings and his longing to be back home, "in the Oklahoma hills where I belong."

Many months have come and gone, since I wandered from my home,
In the Oklahoma hills where I was born.
Many pages of life have turned, many lessons I have learned,
Since I wandered from those hills where I belong.

CHORUS:
Way down yonder in the Indian nation, ridin' my pony on the
reservation,
In the Oklahoma hills where I was born.
Way down yonder in the Indian nation, a cowboy's life is my
occupation,
In the Oklahoma Hills where I was born.

With that tearful, longing look in his eyes, it was clear what our future would hold. One day we would move back to the Oklahoma hills where he belonged. That became our long range goal; one that we would work toward, and look forward to, for the next twenty years.

As the Maestro conducted the song over and over, each time we heard it, we would be carried off to that dreamland place, the Oklahoma hills where we belonged.

Philippians 1:8 *"God can testify how I long for all of you with the affection of Christ Jesus."*

A New Song

Over the years I had written some music, lyrics, and parodies, but it was nothing that came naturally or easily. I worked very hard at it, spending hours at the piano perfecting the melody, then immediately writing down the notes and lyrics for fear I would soon forget them.

One Sunday morning in September, 1999, the great Maestro gave me my own cue. I woke up with a new song in my head and heart. This was something special and quite different. I had the entire melody and all the lyrics to a song in my head. It felt like an old song I had known for a long time, but it wasn't, it was new.

I got out of bed, went downstairs, sat at the piano and played the entire piece. This too was something I had never done before. After years of playing the piano, I could learn to play a piece if I practiced it, and I could improvise on a melody line if I had the chords, but what I did that morning was far beyond my capability. It's hard to explain, but it was as if someone was playing this new song through my hands. I remember sitting at the piano that morning in shock over the experience.

We went to church as usual, and that afternoon Jack had a church finance committee meeting to attend. I went along as we had plans to go to supper with some friends after the meeting.

While he was in the meeting, the melody resurfaced in my mind. I grabbed a piece of copy paper, quickly drew some music staffs on it and headed for the piano in the auditorium. To my surprise I could once again play the entire piece without printed sheet music. Amazed, and yet afraid I would forget it, I quickly jotted down the melody line, chords, and lyrics. While playing through it one last time, a friend of mine came in to listen. Being a singer, she asked me about the new song she had obviously never heard before.

I knew the song was a gift from God because it was far beyond anything I was capable of doing myself. However not wanting her to think I was nuts, I simply said it was something I had just written. She said she liked it very much, and perhaps she could sing it at some point.

Tomorrow would bring more from the Maestro.

Psalm 33:3 *"Sing to him a new song, play skillfully, and shout for joy."*

More to Come

J ack got up early the next morning and left for work as usual. As I arrived at the lumber yard about 8:30 AM, I noticed one of the trucks loaded and parked in the front lot. When I walked through the door, Jack asked me if I had anything special I had to do that day. Upon my response of "No," he promptly handed me the paperwork and told me to jump in the truck and take the load to North Kern State Prison in Bakersfield, which was at least an eight hour round trip.

I liked to drive so I was happy for the opportunity to go. I always took a yellow lined pad with me when I drove the truck, because sometimes I would get ideas about things and I would want to write them down.

In no time I was on the road headed south on Hwy 99 to Bakersfield. I had not driven ten miles, when another song began to come into my head. To write music without playing it on the piano was something I had never done before, but I did my best to write it on the yellow pad, complete with the lyrics. Wow, another whole song! By the time I arrived in Bakersfield this second song was down on paper, and once again I was in shock.

On the way back from Bakersfield, here came song number three. Again I wrote it down as best I could, words and all; three songs in two days. To say the least, this was unbelievable, and nothing short of a miracle!

When I arrived home that evening, I saw another truck loaded and parked in front of our house. Jack was outside feeding the cows and horses so I sat down at the piano. Much to my surprise I could easily play the two new songs!

When Jack came in he told me he needed me to get up really early the next day and take the load that was on the truck to the prison in Susanville. Now this was a really long trip; eight hours each way. I would have to leave by 3:00 AM the next morning.

I was always willing to do whatever it took to make our business a success, so I set the alarm for 2:30 AM and went to bed early.

I didn't know it, but the Maestro was just getting warmed up.

Deuteronomy 30:20 *"...listen to His voice, and hold fast to Him."*

A Lot More

On the long trip to Susanville, you guessed it, more music; two more songs. I was so amazed by what had transpired in the last two and a half days I could not even remember unloading the truck in Susanville.

Eight hours in the truck going home brought more. Not more music, but a story line to go with the music. By this time I was not questioning anything coming to my mind. I simply wrote it down on the yellow pad that sat on the seat beside me.

It came in short phrases with brief, quick ideas that I could easily write down without driving off the road. Piece by piece the story unfolded as God revealed to me what He needed to say. Faithfully, I put it down on the yellow pad.

Characters, scenes, personalities, props, costumes, everything about it was coming into my head in small snippets. One or two words painted a detailed picture in my mind. The words made their way to the yellow pad, while the picture and all the details remained in my head. I knew by now that I would not be forgetting a single thing about this. God would not allow it.

One at a time, He placed pictures in my mind, I wrote a couple of words down on the yellow pad, and then filed that picture away in my memory bank to be easily recalled at a later time.

As my trip progressed, so did the story. The closer I got to home, the faster I wrote. By the time I parked the truck at the lumber yard that night, the outline for a complete story line was down on that yellow pad. I felt like I had been in a three day whirlwind. I wasn't tired, but very excited about what God was doing through me, while wondering all the while, "Why me?"

I knew what God had given me, and I knew what I had to do, but how? How would I do this? I didn't know anything about musical plays except for having played a few parts in high school.

This was to be a brief sonata in my life overture with parts for many new musicians that the Maestro was about to cue one at a time. He had a plan and I had a willing heart.

Exodus 36:2 *"...the Lord had given ability to those willing to come and do the work."*

Divine Gift

O ver the months to come, the play became a project that totally engulfed me. There was so much to do. The dialogue, the script, and the music, not to mention everything it would take to actually bring the whole thing to fruition; first things first, the script.

I had not said much about it to anyone, for fear I wasn't going to be able to finish it. I had never written anything before, so at one point I asked my niece to help me with the dialogue, which she did a little. However, when she wanted to change the story line, I retreated back to working alone. No way was I about to change what God had given me.

I worked feverishly through the fall and winter. Every chance I got was spent on God's play which was on my mind constantly. I know what I am about to say is a double negative, but I simply could not, not do it. I was unable to get it off my mind or out of my heart. God had planted it there, now it was growing into the complete sonata the Maestro had composed for this specific time in my life overture.

The title was something that would not come easily. What did God have in mind? After much prayer, consideration, and thought, it occurred to me that the message of the play was: No matter how tough life gets, we are never alone; thus the title, "Never Alone."

I put the script on the computer, printed it off and put it on a clip board. I carried it with me everywhere I went, constantly tweaking each line. I reviewed it time and time again, making the slightest changes. Each night I would update the script on the computer and print it off again. I could see it come to life on paper as God continued to give me the exact words to write.

Eventually, by February, 2000 I had the whole thing down on paper and had tweaked it for the last time. I had done the very best I could. The script was finished. Now what? Where do I go from here? Where do I begin? God had given this to me and I was determined to do it, but how?

I had no idea, but obviously God had a plan; after all, it was His play.

Isaiah 14:24 *The Lord Almighty has sworn, "Surely, as I have planned, so it will be, and as I have purposed, so it will stand."*

The Read Through

I mustered up the courage to approach my pastor and his wife about it, and they suggested I get some people together and read through it. They agreed to have the "read through" in their home, where they had a piano.

I asked some people who I thought would be interested and they all agreed to participate. As that day approached, the song in my heart became tense with emotion. The butterflies in my stomach were as big as hummingbirds, and the tension within me grew as the nervousness mounted.

Was this really what I thought it was? Was it really from God? Had I written it well? I wasn't much on failure and I didn't want to start now. Every instrument was playing at the same time the song of question and confusion as I loaded the script and music in my car.

It was only a fifteen minute drive to my pastor's home, but it seemed like an eternity. The bass drum pounded out a fast heart beat in my chest. I wanted to go over the script one more time. Perhaps there was still something to add; something to change. There wasn't time, I was there. Parked in front of my pastor's home, I prayed. I thanked God for the opportunity to serve Him in this way, and I pleaded to Him for strength through this process. I was scared to death, not knowing if they would like it, or rip it to shreds.

I was the first to arrive at my pastor's house, and his wife had everything set up for the read through. The chairs were around the table, and she had moved the piano close by. This was it. Months of work lay in front of me in a pile of papers. I had printed off eleven copies of the script, one for each member of the cast, and each part was marked for its reader. We put one copy at each place. One by one the readers came and took their seats around the table. I did my best to appear calm and loose, but I was as tight as a drum.

The script that had been seen by no one but God and me, was now in the hands of eleven people. They were all my friends, and I trusted each one of them. I wanted the truth, and I wanted it to be good. I took my place at the piano. I was ready; extremely nervous, but ready.

My song of self-confidence I knew so well was being drowned out by the tune of vulnerability played in a minor key, which made me fearful of the outcome.

Mark 4:40 *"...Why are you still afraid? Do you still have no faith?"*

Now What?

After prayer, we began to read. Each one seemed to quickly get into their character and read with more enthusiasm than I had expected. The tension broke slightly.

I wondered if they would laugh during the funny parts, feel the sadness when it was called for, and be convicted by the underlying message. It progressed nicely and they didn't rush it. When it came time for a song, I played it on the piano and sang it as best I could.

Yes, they laughed and shed a few tears, as each part was read. I could tell by their demeanor, it drew them in emotionally, and they appeared to be able to follow the story line as it moved from one scene to the next.

When they finished reading and I played the final song, it was over. The silence in the room was deafening. I sat at the piano afraid to ask what they thought. I knew in my heart it was good, it came directly from God. If it needed changes, this was the time to do it. Constructive criticism, that's what it would be, and I could take that.

Finally after what seemed like an eternity, I broke the silence and asked, "Well, what do you think?" "What should be changed?" "Is there any part that is not theologically sound?"

They looked at each other and then at me. Once again the tension mounted within me and I could hear the drum pounding in my chest. Finally, one broke the silence and declared that she thought it was good just the way it was. Okay, so that's one, but what did the others think?

One at a time they each gave their critique. They mentioned the parts they liked best and the song that was their favorite. In the end they each thought it was wonderful just as it was, and no changes should be made.

What a relief. But what did I expect? God wrote it, shouldn't it be good? The first stanza of the sonata was complete. I had made it over the first hurdle and the race was on.

My heart sang a mixed melody all the way home. A song of relief, excitement, and complete puzzlement engulfed my mind. The race was on all right, but on to where? Where would I go from here?

Psalm 25:4 *"Show me your ways, O Lord, teach me your paths."*

Rex Schneider

Now the work would really begin on what would prove to be the most challenging project of my life thus far. The Maestro was in His place on the platform, at the podium with the baton in His hand, and I was not about to try to conduct from my chair.

The cast, the crew, the musicians, the director, the producer, the lighting, the sound……. The list went on and on and I didn't have a clue where to begin.

Once again I went to my pastor who suggested I put a sign-up sheet on the bulletin board for anyone who would be interested in being involved. I took his suggestion, and posted the sign-up sheet the following Sunday.

That morning as I sat in worship service I noticed a young man who was new to the church. He played the guitar and could sing very well. I didn't know who he was, but God encouraged me to introduce myself to him after the service. I've never been one to just walk up to someone cold, but I knew I would have to if I was to find out who this young man was, and if he might be interested in taking part in the play.

When the service ended, I walked straight up to him, introduced myself and he told me his name was Rex. I expressed that it was obvious he was a very talented young man and I wondered if he might be interested in being involved in a musical play I had recently written.

In a matter of seconds, the look on his face went from dumbfounded to the biggest smile I had ever seen. Then he said, "I knew God sent us to this church for a reason." It seems that he and his wife

Suzie, and their four children, had just begun coming to our church. Rex was a man who tried his best to live by the Spirit and go where the Spirit led him. He felt they had been led to attend this church, even though it was a long distance for them to drive.

The Spirit had led them there alright, and this musical play was one of the reasons. The Maestro had just cued the most important person in the show.........Rex Schneider.

Galatians 5:25 *"Since we live by the Spirit, let us keep in step with the Spirit."*

God is Good!

As we stood talking, Rex explained to me that he and his family had recently moved to our area from the Northwest. Then he let go a trumpet blast that I never expected to hear. He humbly shared with me that he was quite familiar with the inner workings of musical plays. What he was telling me was the music to my ears I never dreamed I would hear from a single person.

Rex had been involved in many musicals and dramatic productions. He knew how to block scenes, direct the cast, and produce an entire show. He also knew about sound systems, lighting, make-up, costumes, and character development. Not only could he sing and act, he had the knowledge to completely organize the whole production.

Rex shared with me his abilities as I listened in total amazement. He wasn't the least bit boastful; he was simply telling me about his past experiences and his love for dramatic productions.

God is good! He had completely prepared Rex for this, and sent him here to our little church. I later learned that the Schneiders had been moving to our area at exactly the same time I was writing the play. God had provided a good job for Rex in the area, and they were able to quickly find an affordable home to rent that suited their rather large family.

God's timing is perfect, and the Maestro precisely cues each and every player. This sonata in my life overture called "Never Alone," had been meticulously orchestrated perfectly down to the most intricate detail by the Master Himself.

Rex suggested that casting the parts should be the first thing, so that's what would come next. The never failing Maestro had the baton in His hand ready to give the cue to the woman who was destined to play the lead role.

Ecclesiastes 8:6 *"For there is a proper time and procedure for every matter..."*

Michelle Hise

The lead role in the show was the most important one. This woman would have to be a good actress and a very good singer. Among the songs she would sing, would be the very first song I woke up with in my head that Sunday morning over six months earlier. The song required a big, strong, expressive, and soulful, alto voice.

That same Sunday morning a young woman sang a special in church. I had never seen her before and had no idea who she was, but boy could she sing. In fact she had the perfect voice for the lead role.

After church I asked our Music Director about her. He told me she was a school teacher named Michelle Hise, and she and her family had recently begun coming to our church. I asked him for her phone number which he gave me without question.

The very next day, on my way home from work, I called her on my cell phone and she answered on the first ring. I introduced myself and told her how much I enjoyed her special music at church the day before. After she thanked me, I popped the question. I explained to her that I had written a musical play and wondered if she might be interested in participating. I also mentioned that she had the perfect voice for the lead role.

Hesitating due to her shock, she finally spoke and shared with me that her minor in college was drama, which was really her passion. Her teaching job was just that, a job.

By this point she was stunned and so was I; first Rex and now Michelle. This could not be a coincidence, it was too perfect. God was all over this project and I knew it.

She jumped at the chance to have the lead role of Ruth, and wanted to meet with me as soon as possible to go over the script and the music. The most important role had been cast; one down and ten to go.

1 Corinthians 14:40 *"...everything should be done in a fitting and orderly way."*

And Phil Makes Three

T hat week I met with Michelle at her home. I brought her a copy of the script and the music. When I played the first song for her, she fell in love with it. It was as if it had been written for her voice, and she could sing it perfectly after hearing it only once. Her part required that she sing several songs. She was an excellent vocalist and all the songs she would be singing presented no problems for her.

We read through the script and I played the songs as they came up. Michelle's husband, Phil, was there and he was all ears listening to every word and song. I knew he was a school principal, but what I didn't know until then was that he was also a musician. He played the trombone quite well and some other brass instruments too.

After hearing the play and songs, he expressed an interest in helping orchestrate the music. This was an area where I really needed help and Phil had some experience along these lines. All I had down on paper was the melody lines and chords. I could play the songs off this, but I knew no one else could, and the music would have to consist of far more instruments than just the piano, since the songs were all quite different. Phil was the man for the job, and the Maestro had just given him the cue.

Excitement filled the room as we discussed what was ahead of us. Yes it would be work, but we could do it, and it was going to be great!

When I left their house that day, my load was much lighter and my song considerably brighter. I had enlisted the help of Rex,

Michelle, and Phil. Things were looking up, but there were still a lot of parts to be cast and a tremendous amount of work to be done.

The flutes and piccolos were alive with excitement of what had just occurred, but the questioning tune was still being played by many other musicians as I wondered how, and if, this play would make it to the stage.

Ephesians 4:16 *"...each part does its work."*

Cast and Crew

Next Sunday when I arrived at church I went immediately to the bulletin board to check the sign-up sheet. Much to my surprise there was quite a list of people who signed up expressing interest in being involved in the play.

Some names were familiar and some I had never seen before. I was thrilled! That morning I made contact with those I knew, and that afternoon I called the rest to tell them of the first meeting which was to be that week.

At that meeting, we discussed who would have each part and who would fill other crew positions. I was amazed at how smoothly it all went, and by the time the meeting was over, every cast position had been filled and there were plenty of others who were happy to help with everything else.

I gave each cast member their copy of the script and the rehearsal schedule, which would be pretty grueling if we were going to meet our performance date of late September. Everyone was in agreement to learn their lines and music, and make all the rehearsals.

We were off and running, but the music was still a problem. Rex was a computer whiz and he told me about a computer program that would actually write sheet music from what was played on an electric piano. I had an electric keyboard but I really didn't like it because it was too small. I went to the music store and bought a full size electric piano and ordered the program Rex told me about.

The program arrived quickly and I began to write the sheet music. This program was amazing. Whatever I played on the piano immediately appeared in the form of sheet music on the computer screen.

From that I could transpose it into other keys or make changes to it if I needed to. In one evening I had all the sheet music done. It was one of the easiest parts of the whole project.

It was all coming together nicely and my orchestra was now playing what would soon be the overture for "Never Alone."

Proverbs 16:3 *"Commit to the Lord whatever you do and our plans will succeed."*

Show Time!

We rehearsed all summer and were right on schedule. Rex had the know-how and I had the want-to. God had blessed me with the financial resources to rent the lighting equipment, sound systems and microphones needed for the production.

I worked on costumes, publicity, programs, and anything else that needed to be done while I was not at work at the lumber yard. It seemed as though the whole church family at Country Oaks Baptist Church was involved in some way. Men were making props, musicians were practicing, the cast was memorizing their lines, and people were buzzing around everywhere as we worked to pull it together.

Everyone was as ready as possible. There was no more practicing, no more tweaking, no more time for memorizing. We would go on and pray that God would bless whatever weak moments popped up and that the audience would not notice if something went wrong.

The week of the show we rented all the lighting and sound equipment, and Rex knew how to set it all up and instruct the people in their positions. The night before the first performance was full dress rehearsal, and it went off without a hitch!

Finally it was show time! People in our community came in droves and it was a roaring success. We did five performances in three days, so by Sunday evening we were all exhausted as the Maestro brought the curtain down for the last time.

This sonata that rang out for over a year in my life overture, faded away into the distance. The lighting and sound equipment were returned, the costumes were boxed up, the props torn down, and the scripts put away. It was finished.

God had blessed me with a wonderful gift. The gift of a musical play called "Never Alone," and He had provided every person needed to make it happen. This gift blessed many people who made up the audience as well as the cast, crew, and musicians. It was a passage in my life overture that was exciting and rewarding all at the same time, and I feel blessed that God entrusted it to me.

My heart sang another song of accomplishment, but could barely be heard over my song of praise. It was an accomplishment, but I never really felt like it belonged to me. I knew it belonged to God from the day He put the first song in my heart, and all the glory was His, and His alone.

Psalm 40:3 *"He put a new song in my mouth, a hymn of praise to our god. Many will see and fear and put their trust in the Lord."*

Happy Birthday

Jack's sister Betty, as well as several of our friends, had Jack Russell Terrier dogs, cute little things with lots of energy and very, very smart. I enjoyed visiting the owners of the little terriers, and playing with their dogs.

On October 21, 2001, my 51st birthday, Jack and I worked at the lumber yard as usual, and at the close of the day, Jack told me that he had a delivery to make on the way home and he would be a little late. This was nothing out of the ordinary, as we often made deliveries after work; sometimes well into the night to fulfill commitments to customers.

I went home and started to prepare our dinner. About 7:30 PM I heard Jack's truck pull into the driveway. He came in the house and announced that my birthday present was out in the truck. He added, "Go out and get it. It's in a brown paper bag on the floor of the passenger seat." Well, I thought, "Don't go out of your way to have it gift wrapped, not to mention bring it in the house."

Feeling a little put out, I went outside where he parked the truck. When I opened the passenger door, there it was, just like he had described it, a brown paper grocery bag, with the top rolled closed. I reached down to pick it up and it moved. I stepped back thinking Jack was playing one of his practical jokes on me again. I turned around, and there he was with a big smile on his face. "Go ahead, look inside." I carefully opened the bag, and there inside was the cutest little Jack Russell puppy I had ever seen. As fast as I opened it, I closed it up again. I turned to Jack and promptly told him that I did not want that dog. In all of our years of marriage, Jack never allowed an animal in our house. It didn't matter if it was sick, dying, or what, it wasn't coming in the house. I knew this little dog would freeze to death with winter coming soon. I would rather not have a Jack Russell Terrier than have my heart broken.

Jack took me by the shoulders, looked me straight in the eyes and said, "I know the dog needs to be in the house. You can have it in the house." You could have knocked me over with a feather. I couldn't believe what I was hearing. Then he added, "There are going to be times in your life when you need companionship." What in the world did he mean by that? I didn't know, and I didn't care. I had a Jack Russell Terrier puppy, and before long the little dog had a name: Duncan.

Duncan brought such joy to my life and a new song to my overture; the sweet, light melody of puppy love and all the joy that came with the little ball of fur.

Proverbs 18:16 "*A gift opens the way for the giver and ushers him into the presence of the great.*"

Duncan

Retired

Over the years we traveled back to Oklahoma as often as we could and with every trip, our goal became stronger and our dream of one day living there became closer to a reality.

It was the fall of 2001. We had just celebrated Jack's 60th birthday and the world was changing. 9/11 had just happened, and California's economy was going down hill fast. The rules, regulations, taxes, and bureaucracy that went along with owning a small business were becoming more than we could bear. Jack made the decision that the time had come to sell the lumber yard.

This would bring an end to a forty-two year career for him. I know it was not a decision he made easily. However, it was his to make, and I would trust this decision, just as I had trusted all his decisions for the last twenty-seven years.

In addition to us both working full time at the lumber yard, we had quite a large cattle operation going, and I had been doing a considerable amount of catering. Also, we were quite active in our local community and church. Needless to say, every musician in the pit was playing their heart out in competition to be heard. The pace of the music was swift, energetic, and approaching hectic allegro, but once again the Maestro was about to wave the baton and make a well needed change in the pace.

We listed our business and it sold almost immediately; resulting in our retiring from the lumber business by May of 2002. A melody that had played for a very long time had ended. The chorus of telephones, forklifts, saws, and delivery trucks would no longer be heard.

Our overture would take on a little slower pace, but between family, cattle, catering, church activities, service organizations, and community commitments, it was anything but muted and dull.

Ecclesiastes 3:13 *"That everyone may... find satisfaction in all his toil—this is the gift of God."*

Jack

Faith That Never Failed

In July of 2002, the Maestro would wave the baton and put an end to one of the most beautiful parts of my life overture.

On Sunday morning, July 29, 2002 we stopped to pick up my mother-in-law, Ruby, and take her to church with us as we did each week. This week would be different as she announced that she wasn't feeling well and did not want to go.

This was highly unusual, so after church we stopped by again to check on her. We found her to be worse and took her to the emergency room at the hospital.

Four hours later the Maestro ended Ruby's song forever. A perforated bowel had filled her with an infection she was unable to fight. There was nothing the doctors could do.

Ruby was almost 96 years old, but her death came as a shock to everyone. It left a hole in the heart of the family that would never be filled.

Ruby's song of faith that never failed, her sweet smile, generous heart and warm nature, had become such an important part of my life overture. For over twenty-five years she lived less than 1/4 mile away from us on our ranch. She was a wonderful mother, grandmother, great-grandmother, friend, and the greatest mother-in-law I could ever hope for.

I learned a lot from Ruby Betts in the 29 years I knew her. She was a beautiful person and the best example of a Christian I have ever known in my life. She never possessed much of earthly value, but she earned many stars for the crown that she will wear in Glory for ever and ever.

With a wave of the baton the Maestro brought an end to her earthly song, but I know she is singing a new song in Heaven, as she glorifies her Lord and Savior she loved so much here on earth.

If I listen real close, I can still hear her sweet song playing in the archives of my heart.

Proverbs 31:31 *"Give her the reward she has earned, and let her works bring her praise at the city gate."*

Oklahoma

B y the end of 2002 it had become apparent to both Jack and I that there was nothing to keep us in California. Our daughter had moved to Idaho, taxes and the cost of living were increasing, and our freedoms were decreasing.

In January 2003 we made a trip to Oklahoma in search of a ranch to purchase. Jack's cousin, Perry Ray, had died the prior year. His wife, Carol, needed to sell their place in Caney, which was part of a 480 acre ranch Perry and his brother, Tinker, were partners in. During this period, Tinker was having a difficult time managing both his ranch and Perry's.

We were familiar with Perry and Carol's place as we had stayed with them on occasion in years past. It was a good piece of productive ranch land and Jack knew it would serve his cattle operation well.

The house, on the other hand, was very small and very old. It would never work for us, but to build a new home was nothing new, we had built our last three homes. There was another little house on the property that we could remodel and live in while we were under construction on our new home.

After some discussion and looking at another ranch, we struck a deal with Tinker and Carol and bought the ranch in Caney. The only draw back to the whole deal was that it was eighteen miles from Ward's Chapel, and there was no doubt Ward's Chapel was where we would be attending church. To be a part of Ward's Chapel was one of the most important things to Jack. He spent the first 10 years of his life there, was baptized there, and his dream was to spend the rest of his life there. If it was Jack's dream, it was my dream.

We traveled ten miles to church every Sunday in California, so eight more miles wouldn't be a problem. Besides, Tinker and Carol really needed to sell. In addition, if we bought the ranch, it would stay in the family.

The decision was made, and with the stroke of our pen and the wave of the Maestro's baton, the page was turned on our life overture. Our dream of living in Oklahoma was about to become a reality.

Mark 5:19 *"...Go home to your family and tell them how much the Lord has done for you, and how he has had mercy on you."*

The Move Begins

J ack was so excited he could hardly stand it. As soon as we got back to California he couldn't wait to share the news with all his friends. His dream was coming true. He would be headed back to those Oklahoma Hills where he was born, and where he belonged.

His friends didn't share in his excitement. They loved Jack so much; it would be hard to see him go. They had been friends for years, and they didn't understand what was so special about Oklahoma. Why would anyone want to live there? Jack assured them once they came to visit and they could fish and hunt on the ranch, they would understand what was so special about Oklahoma. He made it a little easier for them to swallow, but they still didn't think much of the idea. Their best friend was leaving.

In early February, 2003 Jack and I made the first trip which began the long process of moving all the animals and ranch equipment to Oklahoma. Over the next four months we made ten trips together back and forth, each time moving more cattle and equipment to what would be our new home, our dream home.

We were very active at our church and with community events in California, so during this time of moving we always managed to be in California on weekends. It was important to us we fulfill our commitments there until we were officially moved. Then we would transfer community loyalties to Atoka County and our church membership to Ward's Chapel, where we would serve the rest of our days.

Back and forth we traveled the 1,755 miles between our two ranches. While in Oklahoma, Jack would work on the fences and barns, and I worked to remodel the little house that would serve as our temporary home while we built our new house. In California, Jack got the next load ready to go, took care of his cattle, and consoled his friends whose crying was becoming louder by the day over his soon departure. I stayed busy staging our house to be sold, which was a huge job. Everything personal had to be packed in boxes, and the entire house had to be painted inside and out.

During the spring and early summer of 2003, the familiar buzz of work, mixed with the hum of truck tires played fast and furious, as we traveled east and west from California to Oklahoma and back. Our overture played the tunes of packing, bawling cows, painting, power tools, tractors, and truck engines all at the same time.

Judges 7:13 *"...a man was telling his friend his dream...."*

Take Two

While at church one Sunday, our pastor mentioned to me that he would like me to stage a reproduction of "Never Alone" before we moved to Oklahoma. As if I wasn't hearing enough different songs all already. "Never Alone" again? What was he thinking? This would take a lot of work, and to pull it off in a short time was questionable. The next Sunday he mentioned it again, only this time it was almost as if he was insisting I do it.

Not to be disrespectful, I made some phone calls to the cast members and musicians, some of whom no longer attended our church. I also called Rex Schneider who had moved his family back to Oregon. Some of the cast said, "Yes," and some said, "No." Rex, however said he would love to come back and help us if I needed him to. If I needed him? That was a given; I needed him alright. Without Rex I couldn't have done it the first time, and I surely wouldn't be able to do it again.

With some changes to the cast, musicians, and crew, we set out to do "Never Alone" one more time. Unlike the first time, I would not always be available. I told them they were going to have to set their own rehearsal schedule and pull it together on their own.

Remarkably, all the props were still intact, and after two and a half years, the cast still remembered their lines quite well. I had the original rental agreements for the lighting and sound equipment, so to rent them again would be no problem.

The cast, crew, and musicians put it together in just over four weeks. In March, 2003, it was "Never Alone (take two)" at Country Oaks Baptist Church, in Elk Grove, California. The repeat performance brought much of the same results as the first, and the hearts of many were blessed.

The Maestro cued my orchestra to again play all the songs from "Never Alone" which brought back so many wonderful memories.

2 Peter 1:12-13 "So *I will remind you of these things…..it is right to refresh your memory…."*

Peace and Quiet

In 2003 the real estate market in California was hotter than a fire-cracker. It was a sellers market, and the perfect time to be moving property. Typically, any listing would sell within a week and would have multiple buyers who would bid up the property until eventually one buyer would win out.

Due to the market situation, Jack decided that we would not list our home until we had all the animals and ranch equipment moved and had the little house in Oklahoma remodeled enough to live in. There was no way we were going to list our house, have it sell right away, and be without a place to live. That just didn't make sense, besides there was a lot of work to be done before we could list it.

By the first of May we were at the point where we could put our California place on the market. Jack was confident that even if it sold immediately, we could insist on a thirty day escrow which would give us enough time to make the final move. Most of the animals were in Oklahoma, and the little house was close enough to being livable. Our house in California was perfectly staged to sell and we were confident, given the current market conditions, a sale was imminent.

Every day we moved closer and closer to meeting our goal and fulfilling our dream. Jack would often share his longing to enjoy the ranch and his cattle, without having to be in a hurry to go some-where or do something.

Jack wanted to watch the ten day old baby calves jumping and bucking with their tails straight up in the air, running circles around their mothers and then finding the security and safety of being by her side, as they drink the nourishing milk she provides. He sought peace in the sight of a group of calves curled up, asleep in the sunshine under the watchful care of a single cow, while the other mamas feed nearby, or just watching a herd of cows as they graze on the tall grass that grows so plentifully in the river bottom ground. There is nothing more peaceful than to sit in the stillness of the early morning light, and watch a herd of cattle while they graze.

This had to be the next passage the Maestro would have for our life overtures. It was the song we both so desperately longed to play; "Peace, Quiet and Contentment."

1 Timothy 2:2 *"...that we may live peaceful and quiet lives in all godliness and holiness."*

Jack and his cattle

On the Road Again

We listed our home and went on about our moving process and work in Oklahoma, expecting the phone to ring at any time to hear our realtor say he had several offers on our house, and they were in a bidding war. However, there was no activity on our place at all; not as much as a looker, let alone an offer. I began to get a little worried, but Jack simply said, "Don't worry, it will sell when it sells."

In the meantime, our plan continued, and our new tune was "On the Road Again." While on the road again, we would discuss what our new home would be like, and how we wanted it to be. As Jack drove, I made simple drawings on a yellow pad depicting our ideas. Our home would be functional and nice, but by no means, pretentious. Neither one of us liked such homes. We also made plans for a one bedroom guest house to accommodate the visitors we knew we would have. Over the years we entertained many people in our California home, and we figured it was sure to increase once we made the move.

Once in Oklahoma, the simple drawings I made on the yellow pad would be transferred to the house plans that were rolled up, standing in the corner, waiting for the next set of additions and corrections. Drawing plans is something I learned to do while working at the lumber yard, and I enjoy it very much.

During those many hours on the road, we would talk for hours at a time as we shared our ideas and dreams of what life in Oklahoma would be like. It was different there and would be a new life, a new culture, and a much slower pace. We were both ready to slow down a bit after the hectic California lifestyle we had lived for so many, many years.

We planned how we would spend our mornings sipping coffee as we sat under that big oak tree on the top of the hill that overlooked the beautiful bottom land of our new ranch. There we could discuss what lay ahead for that day, as we watched the sun break the horizon in the east, and witness the beginning of another day God would give us together.

Jack would reach across the truck seat, take my hand firmly in his, and with that warm inviting smile that came so easily to him, he would say, "It's going to be good. It's all going to be good."

Numbers 10:29 *"...the Lord has promised good things.."*

On the Road Alone

There were times that required Jack and I to drive separate vehicles from California to Oklahoma. When Jack decided he needed his little four wheel drive ranch truck in Oklahoma more then he needed it in California, the next trip meant I would be driving the little truck alone.

Jack loaded it with our big sprayer and some other ranch stuff and I was off and running. Just me, my little dog Duncan, and of course, my trusty yellow pad and pencil. It didn't take long before I knew this was going to be a very long trip. No air conditioning, no radio or tape player, and very uncomfortable hot, sweaty, vinyl seats. The seventeen hundred fifty-five mile trip would seem like five thousand before it ended.

To pass the time I started singing. Somewhere across the desert, I began to sing Patsy Cline's old song, "I Cry Myself to Sleep Each Night." As I sang it, God began to fill my head with some new lyrics for it. It came quite easily and I quickly jotted it down on the yellow pad.

I had just completed a Bible study course on gratitude, so with grateful thoughts fresh in my mind, I wrote:

I pray myself to sleep each night, the Lord's Prayer I first recite,
Then I thank the Lord for blessing me.

I list the things I'm grateful for; every night there's something more,
Everything I have, He gave to me.

Good friends, my church, my family, these I'm grateful for,
My health, His guidance, and His Word, Oh there's so much more.

And so each night before I sleep, I thank the Lord for blessing me,
Everything I have, He gave to me.

Over and over again while driving, I sang the simple parody God had just put in my head. I liked it, but as it says itself, "there's so much more." I knew there had to be more, but I just couldn't put the words together in my mind. Nothing more came. Somewhere in my head there had to be a second verse; there just had to be.

Nothing more came of the simple parody while on that trip. If God had something else to say, He would give it to me. I knew that, and I would be patient.

Psalm 40:1 *"I waited patiently on the Lord;..."*

New Life

It was early June, 2003 when the Maestro added the new, bright, quick tones of the piccolo to my life overture.

My ever present theme song of work was in the foreground as I did my best to convert an old, broken-down, dilapidated house into a place where Jack and I would call home for a short time. It wasn't the first old home I had fixed up for us to live in, but it was the most challenging.

Jack was somewhere on the ranch, and I was in the little house with a paint roller in my hand. At that time there was minimal, if any cell phone service at our place in Oklahoma. We had to stand in the middle of the road to receive a signal, but somehow, on that day the slightest signal got through, and my cell phone made a weird sound like it was trying to ring. I dropped the paint roller and quickly picked up my phone making a mad dash through the front door and outside to the middle of the road where I answered it. It was my daughter, Michelle, calling from Idaho, and I could tell by her voice she was up to something.

She said she had some news for me, and asked if I was sitting down? I answered, "No, I'm standing in the middle of the road so I can hear you." I didn't know whether to be excited or alarmed, so I just listened, as she made the announcement I thought I would never hear. She was pregnant!

Was it April Fool's Day? No, it was early June. How could this be? Michelle was almost 32 years old, and had been married for over twelve years. She had been told over and over again, by several very good doctors, that she would never be able to have any children. You can imagine my surprise at her news. I was thrilled beyond words, until she told me the rest of the story.

The doctors told her that this would be an extremely high-risk pregnancy. After careful examination, they discovered she had a large fibroid tumor growing in her uterus that would most likely out-grow the baby and kill it. My heart sank, and the momentary joy I felt turned to sadness. The beautiful piccolos stopped as quickly as they began, and the mournful drone of the double bass filled my heart.

Michelle had hope far greater than me. She believed this child would survive and be born healthy. Jack and I were both cautiously excited about this child that was scheduled to come into the world the following February. If it was to be, it would be.

2 Timothy 1:12 *"...I know whom I have believed, and am convinced that he is able to guard what I have entrusted to him..."*

One More Trip

B y the end of June everything was coming together very nicely in Oklahoma. The plans for our new home we would build on the site where Perry and Carol's house still stood were complete and so was the plan for the guest house.

Everything was going according to plan except one thing; our house in California had not sold. Not a nibble or even a low offer; nothing. It had been on the market now for almost sixty days, which was unheard of at that time. Even our realtor was baffled by it.

Again Jack said, "Don't worry; it will sell when it sells." Like his mother, Jack was not one to worry about things.

We began taking steps to become established in the community. We met with the owner of the lumber yard in Atoka, and discussed his supplying the lumber and building materials for our new home. We rented a P.O. Box at the Caney Post Office, opened a checking account at the local bank, and sat down with the insurance agent and bought a policy on our ranch.

By the middle of July, the only thing left of the ranch in California was five bulls. Jack had been putting off hauling them because they were rather mean and liked to fight with each other. He wasn't looking forward to them fighting in his trailer for 27 hours, but they had to come. He decided he would make a fast trip to California, rest up for a couple of days, load the bulls in the trailer and drive them back straight through without stopping.

I would stay in Oklahoma and put the final touches on the little house so we could begin staying there when he returned. We had made the trip so many times it was almost like a commute to work, stopping at the same places along the way each time to eat and for fuel.

I watched as he pulled out and headed west for the last time. Although we had made trips driving individual vehicles, this would be the first trip he made alone, and my orchestra played a mixed medley of tunes as I stood waving good-bye until he was completely out of sight. The song of relief that this would be the last trip hauling animals, combined with the minor key tune of concern for his safety, clashed with the sweet melody of our plans for the future, and the wonderful life we had dreamed about for so long.

Lamentations 3:24 "...*The Lord is my portion; therefore I wait for him.*"

Dream Coming True

Whie Jack was making this last trip, I worked tirelessly on the little house. I wanted to make it as nice as possible, since we would be living in it for a time; I hoped a short time. Jack and I knew we should start staying in Caney on the ranch since our cattle and all our equipment was now there. We had been staying at Jack's cousin, Tinker and his wife Elma Lou's house, which was about twenty miles from Caney. Their hospitality was a blessing, but it was time we stayed in our own little place.

We had a cow that had developed hoof rot and while Jack was gone, Tinker came over every day, put the cow in the chute, and gave her a shot, after which he stopped by for lunch and a short visit before heading back to Atoka. It was nice to have company, since I didn't know anyone in Caney yet.

It was Friday, July 18, 2003 and Jack was on his way back with the bulls. His estimated time of arrival would be sometime after midnight, and I was excited. He was making the last trip, and I had the little house livable. I decided to stay there that night and wait for him to get back to the little house which would now be our home. Our place in California was where we used to live.

That night, right on schedule, about 2:00 AM, Jack made it back, unloaded the bulls, and came to the house. Jack never required much sleep, so he was up bright and early as usual the next morning.

After breakfast he got his dogs and headed for the pens to give the sick cow her daily shot. Then he went back to work on the fence he was building. I stayed home to do some things around the little house.

Our total ranch operation had been moved to Caney, and life was good. The Maestro was conducting the song of normalcy, accompanied by the happy refrain of excitement over our plan, and our dream materializing with every passing day.

Philippians 1:6 *"...He who began a good work in you will carry it on to completion..."*

Ward's Chapel Baptist Church

It was Sunday. Excitement and anticipation filled our little house. We would be attending church at Ward's Chapel for the first time. We got up early and Jack went to doctor the sick cow before breakfast. This didn't take long, and he was home to do what he had done every Sunday morning for years: wash the car. Jack always said, "It's just not right to drive a dirty car to church."

I was in our little kitchen fixing breakfast and through the little window I could hear him whistling "The Old Rugged Cross" as he dried and polished our car. This had always been Jack's favorite hymn and I knew he was hoping they would sing it at Ward's Chapel that morning like he recalled doing as a child.

After breakfast we got dressed for church. We were both filled with anticipation. All the family knew we had moved back home and would be in church. We had visited many of them in their homes, but there was something special to Jack about sitting with your family in church, worshiping God together.

They were all descendants of the original families who started Ward's Chapel over one hundred years ago. Many of these people still lived on the original Indian allotment land given to their family generations prior.

Ward's Chapel Church was home, and we were on our way. The eighteen mile drive seemed like fifty as the excitement brewed within us. Jack reached across the seat of our car and took my hand in his. He didn't have to say a word. His faint smile and expressive eyes played the most beautiful rendition of fulfillment, telling me everything I needed to know.

He longed to be back home at Ward's Chapel, and after fifty-three years, he was finally going home, where he would spend the remaining Sundays of his life, worshiping with his family.

Psalm 133:1 *"How good and pleasant it is when brothers live together in unity."*

Ward's Chapel Baptist Church

The Cemetery

It was a very nice service, and we did sing "The Old Rugged Cross." The sound of the bass voices of the Betts men was strong, and Jack was singing his heart out right along with them. I stopped singing, closed my eyes and listened to some of the best harmony of men's voices I had ever heard.

As we sat on that old pew, he took my hand in his and squeezed it tight. I looked in his eyes, and saw a look of total contentment. I had seen a look of contentment on Jack's face before, but nothing could compare to this. We both knew our dream was coming true.

After the service, we were going to Atoka to have lunch with all the cousins. I was driving, and as we approached Ward's Chapel Cemetery, Jack instructed me to pull over and stop. I questioned him about stopping, knowing his family would be waiting for us, but he insisted we stop.

I pulled over, stopped the car, and we got out. He opened the gate for me, and we entered the place we had been so many times before. We knew where all the family gravesites were, but Jack wanted to find them once again.

As we were leaving, he opened the gate for me, and as he did so, he stopped, put his hand on my shoulder and said, "When I die I want to be buried here."

Puzzled by his comment, I reminded him that both his parents were buried in Sacramento, California. He replied, "I know where they're buried, and if I would go ahead and spend the money, I would move them back here where they belong. When I die I want to be buried here at Ward's Chapel, with my people."

The subject of our burial sites was one that we had never discussed in our twenty-nine years of marriage, but I listened as he made his intentions very clear. I could hear the hint of his Native American heritage in his voice that day. It wasn't often, but occasionally it came through, and when it did, I could easily recognize it.

As we drove to meet his family for lunch, he spoke not a word, but the tribal chant of Jack's Choctaw heritage, that he loved so much, played over and over again in my mind and heart.

2 Timothy 1:5 *"I have been reminded of your sincere faith, which first lived in your grandmother...and in your mother..."*

Faith and Hope

M onday morning we got up early, poured a cup of coffee and drove to the top of the hill to sit under the mighty oak tree and watch the sunrise over our ranch.

On the way back to our little house we discussed getting started on our new home. The first thing was a larger electric service, so I agreed to call the electric company and arrange for an engineer to come out. Jack dropped me off and went back to the pens to see about the sick cow that seemed to be improving.

Dusty, the young man who worked with me on the little house, called and said he would be a little late and would be bringing his seven year old daughter Faith, and his eight year old niece, Hope with him. He also said he would not be going to lunch because he would be leaving early to take the little girls somewhere.

At 8:00 AM, I made the call and spoke to the electrical engineer who said he would be able to meet with us on Wednesday at 9:30 AM. When Dusty arrived, the two little girls got out of the truck loaded down with their plastic tubs of craft supplies, and came in the house immediately setting up shop on our tiny kitchen table.

Jack got along with children but he believed they should mind, doing what they are told the first time. He had very little patience with children that did not listen and obey. Consequently, I don't have a lot of good memories of Jack with children.

I knew Jack would be coming home for lunch at 11:30 and would want to sit at our little table and eat. In the twenty-nine years Jack and I were married, he insisted on eating at the table. At 11 o'clock I started making Jack's lunch and the little girls were hard at work at our kitchen table making jewelry. It was very hot outside and I didn't have anywhere to move them and their projects.

I anticipated what Jack would say when he came in, and it wasn't good. I knew he would be hot, sweaty and tired and wouldn't want to listen to two giggling little girls. The closer it got to 11:30 the more nervous I got. I heard Jack's truck drive up. He got out, spoke to Dusty and came to the door. Not having the heart to watch, I didn't even turn around. I heard the door open and Jack say, "Well, who are these two pretty little girls?" Not believing my ears, I spun around and thought, "And who are you in Jack's sweaty clothes?"

He sat down in the third chair at the table between the girls and began talking to them about their projects. They shared with him what they had made and he bragged on their artistic ability. After getting over the shock of what I was witnessing, I asked Jack if he wanted me to have the little girls move so he could sit at the table and eat. "Oh no," he said, "I'll just sit on the couch and eat my lunch on my lap."

I couldn't believe it! I never had seen Jack eat with his plate on his lap. That day he did. When he was finished, he changed his shirt, spoke to the girls again, kissed me good bye, and went back to work.

Work continued that afternoon, and that evening we had Jack's cousin, David Ray, to our little house for supper. My heart sang out my song of hospitality which came naturally to me. David would be the first of many guests Jack and I would entertain in the years to come. I was anxious for our new home to be complete, so we could play the tune of hospitality as a duet, just as we had for so many years in California.

Acts 16:15 *"...If you consider me a servant of the Lord, come and stay at my house...*

Our Special Place

Tuesday July 22, 2003 began once again as we had vowed our days would start, by having coffee under the big oak tree, on the hill, at sunrise. It was such a beautiful spot, and because Jack and I both loved the morning hours so much, we decided we would spend as many mornings as we could at that place; our special place, on our new ranch. We had done it now two days in a row and it felt so good to begin our day together in such a beautiful, peaceful spot.

We stayed there quite a while that morning just talking and reflecting on where we had been and where we were going in life. Jack and I thought alike, so we had a lot of the same hopes and dreams. We enjoyed sharing our thoughts with each other and many times I knew exactly what he was going to say before he even spoke his first word.

As we sat on the hill that morning I felt total peace and contentment and I was in no hurry to go back to the little house. I would have been happy to sit there with him all day. Maybe the day would come when we could just stay up there for a long time watching the squirrels and listening to the various songs of the birds.

The sounds of God's creation were all I heard that morning as Jack put his strong arm around my shoulder and pulled me close to him. As I laid my head on his shoulder in complete contentment, he said, "All I want to do for the rest of my life is work my cows and be a part of Ward's Chapel." We were so happy there in Oklahoma, even if we didn't have a nice house to live in, we had each other and that's all that mattered.

As we walked hand in hand back to the truck that morning, Jack said, "Let's come here every morning if we can; I love this spot." I nodded my head in agreement.

The string section had been playing our love song for over twenty–nine years, and with each year that passed, the Maestro added more depth and volume to the song that so vividly and accurately reflected the love we had for each other.

Song of Solomon 2:3 *"Like an apple tree among the trees of the forest is my lover among the...men."*

Our Tree

I'll See You Later

Wednesday, July 23, 2003 started out as usual except Jack and I did not go to the hill to have coffee and watch the sunrise. He wanted to go and give the cow one last shot and make sure she was okay before turning her out with the other cows.

The electrical engineer would be there at 9:30 AM, to meet with us and Jack had a few other things to do before the engineer arrived. He hugged me tight, kissed me good-bye and said, "I'll see you later." With that he left.

I was working in the kitchen and about 9:30 AM I noticed a pick up pull into the drive way. I quickly determined it was an electric company vehicle, so I walked over to meet him. Jack was not yet there. I introduced myself to the engineer and began telling him of our plans and we discussed what size service we needed and how we would bring it to the site. As we discussed the job, I couldn't help noticing that it was now 9:45 AM and Jack was not there. It was not like Jack to be late for a meeting, especially one that meant so much to us.

I asked the engineer if he would mind if I went back to the house and called Jack on his cell phone. He wasn't in a hurry, so I ran home and made the call. No answer. As I walked back to where the engineer was, I knew something wasn't right. I had that hollow feeling in the pit of my stomach. Something was wrong, very, very wrong.

Again I asked the engineer if he would wait as I drove to the pens where I thought Jack would be, and again he complied with my request, noting that he had some paper work he could do in his truck.

I ran to the house, jumped in our little pick-up truck and headed for the pens which were about a mile away. I pulled up to the double gates and parked. Jack's flat bed truck was there and his two stock dogs were on the back. As I got out of the truck, I noticed that the huge, red cattle chute had fallen over. I jumped over the gate, and as my eyes made their way to the ground, I saw Jack's plaid shirt. Then I saw Jack. He was half buried under the ground with the huge chute on top of him. I ran to him, and realized that what my gut feeling was telling me was true; Jack was gone.

With a wave of the baton, the Maestro brought an end to our beautiful love song that had been the predominant melody of my life overture for almost 30 years.

Ecclesiastes 8:8 *"...no one has power over the day of his death."*

The chute that fell on Jack

The Stranger

I jumped back over the gate, got back in the pick up and drove back to the house where the engineer was working in his truck. I told him what had happened and he said, "Get in my truck, I am a volunteer fireman, and I'll call 9-1-1."

I jumped in his truck and we sped back to the pens, as he called 9-1-1. He pulled his truck up to the double gates, where we both got out and flew over the gate. Together the engineer and I somehow lifted the monstrous chute off Jack and got him out from under it. The engineer immediately went to work on Jack, clearing his air passage and giving him CPR. I knew there was no hope. I knew Jack was gone.

Just then another pick-up pulled up to the gate next to the engineer's company truck. An older man got out and looked over the gate, and never spoke a word. He quietly opened the gates wide, got back in his truck and pulled it into the pen parking it out of the way. He then went back and got in the electric company's truck and moved it out of the way as well.

I stood there watching as the engineer did everything he could to revive Jack. The stranger made his way over to us. He looked down at Jack, and the engineer whose work never ceased. Then the stranger turned to me, and placed both his hands on my shoulders, dropped to his knees, pulling me to my knees. There, he began to pray, and continued praying until we heard the scream of sirens; the ambulance had arrived.

The stranger was the first responder of the Caney Volunteer Fire Department, and to pray for me was his first response. He was Mr.

Joe Crites, one of the finest, Christian men I have ever known. God could have not sent a finer first responder with a better first response.

His prayers that day, brought me the strength I needed to go on; the hardest day of my life. With a wave of the baton, the Maestro had brought total devastation to my life overture.

Romans 15:30 *"...join me in my struggle by praying to God for me."*

Total Silence

The news spread like wildfire, and neighbors and family began to arrive. Jack's cousin Beverly Cochran, was the first family member on the scene. She heard the call come over the radio and got there as fast as she could.

It wasn't long before the paramedics had Jack loaded into the ambulance. I stood with Beverly, totally consumed with grief and disbelief as we looked on. They raced Jack to the hospital in Atoka and Beverly and I followed in her car. I don't remember much about our conversation on the twelve mile trip, but I do remember how kind, caring, and compassionate Beverly was. She was a blessing to me that day, and has been since.

Upon our arrival at the hospital they escorted us to a room that I think was the Chapel, although I'm not sure what it was. Family and friends began coming; everyone was in shock, including me. The room became crowded with people as I sat there numb from the pain.

In addition, several local pastors came and offered their support, each one taking time to pray for me. I knew none of them, but they were doing what the Lord had called them to do; bring comfort to those in their time of need.

After what seemed like hours, a doctor came in and told me what I knew would be the outcome. They had done everything they could for Jack, but were unable to revive him.

There was no more hope. There was no more dream. There was no more reason to live. There was no more Jack. Our love song had come to a close.

With a wave of the baton, the Maestro had brought my life overture to complete silence. The hollowness I felt in the pit of my stomach, carried over to my orchestra. Complete emptiness. No song. No melody. Nothing. Total silence.

Ezekiel 26:13 *"I will put an end to your...songs, and the music of your harps will be heard no more."*

Faith and Strength

Jack and I were both planners and we had spent hours discussing what our life would be like in Oklahoma. We had, as Jack would say, "put the pencil" to our financial situation. We knew our cost of living would be far less in Oklahoma than in California.

Since we owned our own business, we had no retirement income or benefits, which meant we would be responsible for our own health insurance as we had been since 1978 when we went into business for ourselves.

We did have some savings and investments that generated enough income for us to live on. Jack would have been 62 the following month in August, and had applied to begin collecting his Social Security. We figured that we would be just fine.

Jack always provided me with a sense of security when it came to financial matters, but with a wave of the baton, the Maestro changed everything. All the hours we spent discussing and planning meant nothing now. Everything was different.

My situation would appear rather bleak to most people. I was 52 years old. All my livestock and ranch equipment was in Oklahoma on a 480 acre ranch which I was under contract to purchase. All my household goods and furnishings were in California in my home that had not yet sold.

To top it off, I had no income, except what I chose to draw from our investments.

I had to have faith. I had to be strong. I had to survive. I reached down into the depth of my very being and found a strength I didn't know I had. I cried out to God, and He answered.

Psalm 77:1 *"I cried out to God for help; I cried out to God to hear me."*

PART TWO

Revelation: The Blessings

Banished

As I sat in the Atoka Hospital that afternoon, I felt as though my life overture had ended. Our orchestras had played such a beautiful duet of love together, in perfect harmony for so many years; I had forgotten I had my own. Our love song duet was over, but there were many more pages in my score, and the Maestro had plans for much more music in my overture.

It would be a completely new segment with new musicians and new melodies, to be played in keys I had never heard before. The Maestro had already made eye contact with the musicians and they were on the edge of their chairs ready and waiting for his cue to play their part in this new, and exciting segment, which would be called: "Revelation—The Blessings"

In the book of Revelation in the Bible, John was banished to the island of Patmos. During this time of solitude, God revealed to him tremendous visions that would bring revelation to a world of believers. Through these visions God demonstrate that He is in control of both the present and the future. He offers hope and assurance that in the end Christ will achieve victory over Satan who is doomed to eternal punishment.

Like John, I felt like God had banished me to a desert island; the Island of despair. He had my full attention and He was about to show me great things. I would discover wonderful revelations and blessings. Some of these wonders I would recognize immediately, while others the Maestro would wait to give the cue until the precise moment I needed the encouragement and comfort the blessing would bring.

This segment of my life overture, like the rest, had been precisely orchestrated by God, and the Maestro wasted no time with His cue to begin. He turned the page on my overture score, and with a wave of the baton, the first song of blessing would be revealed to me.

Amos 3:7 *"Surely the Sovereign Lord does nothing without revealing His plan to His servants."*

Tinggggg of Hope

After giving me the horrible news about Jack, the doctor asked me the question he was required to ask, "What funeral home do you want to use?"

I had no idea how to respond. I didn't even know what was available. My eyes turned to Tinker for help. With tears in his eyes he responded, "Browns." I turned back to the doctor with the same response, "Browns."

The doctor expressed his condolences to me and left the room. Within minutes Eddie Brown, of Brown's Funeral Service in Atoka, was there. He thought it would be best if he and I went back to his office to discuss the arrangements. We sat down at Eddie's desk and he asked the first question, "Where will Jack be buried?"

The Maestro had just cued the first song of blessing. It rang out pure and true in my head. I instantly remembered three days earlier on Sunday afternoon when Jack and I stood at the gate of Ward's Chapel Cemetery and he initiated a conversation on a subject we had never discussed before: Where he wanted to be buried when he died.

It seemed so out of character at the time for Jack to want to stop at the Cemetery, when we on our way to have lunch with all his cousins. It is almost as if he knew he had something to tell me. The answer to Eddie Brown was clear in my mind. Jack had made it quite clear to me just three days prior when he said, "When I die I want to be buried here at Ward's Chapel, with my people."

I immediately realized it was a huge blessing. If we had not had that conversation, I probably would have had Jack's body shipped back to Sacramento, California and buried next to his parents. I didn't have to make that decision; Jack had made it for me.

The only thing that could be heard was a very faint heartbeat from the percussion section which indicated I was barely alive. With this revelation, the Maestro gave the cue for a single "tinggggggggg" of the triangle which resonated from somewhere way in the back. It was the "ting" of hope. God was in my midst. Hope was present.

Proverbs 23:18 *"...surely there is a future hope for you..."*

Ward's Chapel Cemetery

Remembered Words

I sat with Eddie Brown that day and made the arrangements for Jack's funeral. I was operating out of pure necessity and in somewhat of a trance. I was doing what I had to do, and God was supplying the strength for me to put one foot in front of the other. There was no song, only a dull hum that came from the hollow pit of my stomach.

I knew the chore that lie ahead was not going to be easy. I headed home to Caney to our little house to get started. I had a lot of phone calls to make. Who would I call first? How would I tell them the news? How would I get through this? One phone call at a time. One prayer at a time. Lord, give me strength.

The closer I got to Caney, the more I dreaded the thought of walking into that little house knowing the emptiness I would feel. I had worked so hard on that terrible little shack to make it a home for Jack and me. Now, he wasn't going to be there, and he would never be coming home again. Our little house would be empty.

I parked the car, climbed the three stairs and stood on the porch. I couldn't bring myself to go in and face the emptiness I knew was inside. I stood there a long time, and finally after taking a long, deep breath, I inserted the key into the lock. I paused again, then turned the key, and opened the door. The house was not empty! There to meet me, bouncing up and down like a yoyo was Duncan.

The Maestro had waved the baton and given the cue to my wonderful little dog who had become my best friend. Duncan had made every trip from California to Oklahoma and back with us. He never cried or complained about being in the truck for hours at a time. (Which for a young Jack Russell Terrier is a miracle in itself.)

Then the Maestro shared with me the revelation of the blessing He had bestowed upon me. As I stood in the doorway holding Duncan, I was transformed back in time two years, to my 51st birthday when Jack brought Duncan home in a paper bag. It was completely out of character for Jack to buy a house dog, let alone allow it to be in the house.

I then remembered the exact words he used that evening when he said, "There are going to be times in your life when you need companionship." I remembered thinking then, "What did he mean by that?"

I didn't know then, but I knew now. I was going to need companionship, and the time was now. I held little Duncan close and he licked me all over my face. This little blessing, in the form of a dog, brought a smile to my face on a day when I thought I would never smile again.

Ecclesiastes 4:10 *"If one falls down, his friend can help him up..."*

Jack's Dream

With God's help, I pulled myself together and did what I had to do. I made all the phone calls, and began preparing what I would say at Jack's funeral. I had to be strong because that's what Jack would expect from me. He had taught me to be strong and I wasn't going to let him down now on the hardest day of my life.

As I prepared my remarks, the Maestro revealed the next blessing. For twenty years Jack and I had planned to one day retire in Oklahoma where he could enjoy ranching and he could once again be a part of Ward's Chapel Church.

Jack had a dream. He wanted to live out his last days in the Oklahoma hills where he was born, and where he belonged. His Choctaw heritage was very important to him, and he wanted to live the rest of his life within the Choctaw Nation with his people. He loved his family and wanted to be close to them. He wanted to sit with his family in Ward's Chapel Church and worship God with them like he had done as a child. He wanted to live the relaxed lifestyle that only Oklahoma could offer. He wanted to go home, he wanted to stay home, and he wanted to die at home. And home was Oklahoma.

This was Jack's dream. It wasn't complicated or far-fetched. It was direct and to the point, just like Jack was.

As I wrote, I realized God had granted Jack's requests. All of them. Every aspect of his dream for the rest of his life had come to fruition. His dream had come true. He lived out his last days in Oklahoma within the Choctaw Nation, close to his family. He sat with his family and worshiped with them at Ward's Chapel Church the last Sunday of his life. He made it home, and died at home, doing what he loved to do, working his cattle on his own ranch in Oklahoma, where he belonged.

God had blessed Jack with total fulfillment and allowed him to live out his dream. He only lived it for five days, but he lived it. Everything about it came to pass, everything.

Upon receiving this revelation, with tears of loneliness streaming down my face, my heart began to sing a very quiet, timid song of praise. As horrible as it was, I could see God's Hand in it all. The Maestro was there, and He was revealing things to me. Things that were blessings.

Job 17:11-12 *"...the desires of my heart turn night into day; in the face of the darkness... light is near."*

Who Was This Woman?

I made it through Jack's funeral, and his body was laid to rest with his people, at Ward's Chapel Cemetery on July 27, 2003. The little church was packed with family and friends, some of which came all the way from California in support of me, and out of love and respect for their dear friend, Jack.

This was only the first part, I knew what was yet to come would be far worse. Jack's memorial service at our church in California would be the hard part. I had made flight reservations from Dallas, Texas to Sacramento, California, and on Tuesday, July 29, 2003 I drove to the airport in Dallas, checked my bag and made my way to the security check-in line. Putting my purse and carry-on bag on the conveyor belt, I stepped through the metal detector security framework and past the guard with no problem. As I went to retrieve my purse and carry-on I was met by a guard who escorted me to a table to personally search my bags. He quickly dumped out the contents of my purse on to the table.

While packing my things, and thinking of Jack's upcoming memorial service, I thought it would be nice to have some of Jack's personal items there. Without thinking about the security rules and regulations that recently had been put into effect since 9/11, I put together a few of Jack's things that meant so much to him. In fear my luggage might be lost, I simply dropped the few things in my purse.

Among these things was Jack's pocket knife that his dad had given him for his twelfth birthday. Jack loved this knife and had carried it since then. He was never without it.

The guard seized Jack's knife, and as soon as he did, I remembered the new rules. I knew he was going to confiscate it. I began to explain my situation when a tall, black lady approached the table. She had kind eyes, and said to me, "Don't worry, wait here, I'll be right back." Within minutes she was back with a very small box. She took Jack's knife and carefully wrapped it in paper and placed it in the little box. She taped it closed, put a luggage sticker on the box, and said, "I will see to it that it is checked through to Sacramento. You can pick it up with your luggage."

As I walked to the gate I wondered, who was that lady, and how did she know I was flying to Sacramento? How did she get a luggage sticker with my name on it so quickly? Then the Maestro cued the revelation: He loves me, and will send His angels to be by my side in time of need, and to help me. What a blessing!

Genesis 24:40 *"The Lord...will send His angel with you and make your journey a success..."*

Row 2, Seat B

I made my way to the gate where I heard the announcement that this was a sold out flight. I had used air miles to book my flight, and the only seat available at the time was in first class. I looked at my boarding pass for my seat assignment; Row 2, Seat A. I was hoping the person seated next to me would not want to talk, because I was in no condition to be having a conversation with anyone. I boarded the plane and took my seat which was the window seat in the first row. There was no Row 1. The people filed by with all their belongings as I sat wondering who would occupy Seat B next to me. They kept coming, but no one sat down next to me. I heard the flight attendant shut the doors, still Seat B remained empty.

As the plane pushed back from the gate, I was alone in Row 2; thank you God. I would have 2 1/2 hours to plan my remarks for Jack's upcoming memorial service. As I sat there writing, I received the most powerful revelation thus far: The purpose of Jack's life, and the reason for Jack's death.

Jack was a people person. He loved people, and they loved him. He had hundreds of friends in all walks of life as he associated with anyone. He lived the life truth he learned from his mother, "I am no better than anyone else, and no one is better than I am." Jack simply believed that people are different; some rich and some poor. Some saved and some lost. Jack befriended them all, and he had shared his dream of living out his life in Oklahoma with all of them. Jack was a salesman and a storyteller, and could paint a picture with words very well. He had described to all these friends how wonderful life would be in Oklahoma and how he had dreamed of this time for many, many years. He implanted the excitement of his dream into each of them. Now Jack was gone and so was his dream. All these people were completely and totally devastated by his tragic death.

As these thoughts flowed into my mind, the revelation came to me. This was the purpose of Jack's life, and why he had to die so tragically. He spent his life building friendships with hundreds of people, and had shared his dream with all of them. They are all devastated, and they will all be attending this memorial service. Many of them are lost and need to know that Jesus died for them. They need to hear the Good News of the Gospel, and the announcement of Jack's tragic death was their invitation to hear it. They would all be there alright, and it was up to me to make sure they heard it. Now, I was on a mission!

Seat B had not been empty. It was occupied by the Maestro, and with a wave of the baton, I received the revelation that added a spark of life to my song of despair.

Exodus 9:16 "*...I have raised you up for this very purpose...that my name might be proclaimed...*"

On a Mission

W hen the plane touched down in Sacramento, I was the first one off. I immediately retrieved my luggage, including the box containing Jack's pocket knife. My despair had turned to excitement. I had a lot of work to do, and just three short days to do it. A friend picked me up from the airport and asked me where I wanted to go first. I knew exactly where I had to go first; straight to Country Oaks Baptist Church to see our pastor. I had to share with him the responsibilities that lie ahead of him.

I entered the church and went straight to our pastor's office. As I entered, he took one look at me, and collapsed on his desk, crying uncontrollably. He was among the list of Jacks devastated friends. I walked to his desk and tapped him on the shoulder. He looked up at me with tears pouring down his face, and I said, "Pull yourself together, we have work to do."

Surprised at what he had just heard, he sat up and waited for what I was going to tell him next. I explained the revelation I had received, and told him that there would be a lot of people coming to the memorial service on Saturday, and it was up to him to preach the message of his life. A lot of them were spiritually lost and they needed to hear the truth. Jack had done his part, and now it was up to us to do ours.

With that he pulled himself together. The Maestro had just waved the baton at him, and he was now on the same mission as I was. The great commission to share the Good News to the lost.

He asked me how many people would be here, to which I responded, "Probably, 800 or so."

In his slow Louisiana way he said, "Our church only seats 300."

In my quick California way I said, "Well, figure it out because they're coming."

He knew I meant what I said and he better figure it out. He reached across his desk, pulled his rolodex of church members to him and said, "I have some phone calls to make."

The Maestro had begun giving him the cues to make Jack's memorial service what it had to be: The evangelistic opportunity of a lifetime to reach lost souls for Christ.

Colossians 4:4-5 *"Pray that I may proclaim it clearly, make the most of every opportunity."*

Horse Without a Rider

I had my work cut out for me to make this event successful. Jack had lived his life, and given his life, for these people that called him friend. I knew Jack's life had to end tragically, or they may not come to a memorial service, especially one at a church. I knew they were devastated, and would be open to receiving the message if it was presented in the right way. The Maestro began to give me some cues of my own.

Jack's friends all knew that he loved ranching and riding horses. This would be a good theme for the decorations at the service. There was no casket of course, but we could use the communion table, and put a display of fall flowers with some western touches incorporated into it. The florist was a good friend of mine who assured me she could create the perfect floral display.

I had a good, recent photo of Jack which was taken by his friend, Gary Wright, in Oklahoma. It depicted Jack on the ranch, wearing his straw cowboy hat, with the cattle in the background. I would have the photo enlarged and framed, and place it on one end of the table with some of Jack's personal belongings around it. On the other end would be his good boots and felt hat. It would be a nice display, but it wasn't quite enough. There had to be something more. It had to be more dramatic. I needed something that would really tug at their heart as they sat and listened to our pastor preach the message to them. What could it be?

The moment I walked in our house, the Maestro gave me the cue; the large painting Jack loved so much. The one of the lonely horse standing next to a tree all saddled up, with his head drooping down and the reins hanging to the ground. There was no rider; only an empty saddle. This painting hung in our home for years and would be the perfect addition. Jack loved it, and all his friends knew it. I would put it on my dad's wooden easel, and stand it just behind, on the left side of the table display, where everyone could see it. That was it! That's what I would do to create the solemn atmosphere that was needed.

The plan was coming together. It would be good, and Jack's purpose in life would be fulfilled. My heart rejoiced in a song of praise over the love Jack had for all his friends, and the fact that they would soon know the love Jesus has for them as well. A love far greater than their friend Jack could ever have.

Romans 5:8 *"...God demonstrates His own love for us in this: While we were sinners, Christ died for us."*

Photo used at Jack's memorial service

The Memorial Service

Plans for the rest of the memorial service were coming together as well. I went through all our photographs and found as many photos of Jack with his friends and family as I could. I made six huge collages that were set up in various locations. The Elk Grove Rotary Club, where Jack was a member, agreed to cook and serve the meal which would follow the service. Our nephew, Lance Kell, was prepared to sing three songs, in his western style that Jack loved so much. I had prepared the remarks I would make and our pastor was ready to preach his heart out.

The only problem left was how to put 800 people in a church that sat 300. The Maestro had taken care of that a long time ago, but no one knew about the plan until now. It seems there was a family who had recently began attending our church. The husband was an expert in electronics, including audio/video. Also we had a family attending our church who owned a local party rental business. Our pastor arranged to rent a very large tent and five hundred chairs which would be set up in the back parking lot. The gentleman who was knowledgeable in electronics would simulcast the memorial service live into the tent. Every one of the 800 guests who attended Jack's memorial service had a great seat either in the church or in the tent.

It was a heart wrenching and emotional service. I shared my remarks about Jack, followed by our pastor who cried, no he bawled, through his whole message in which he spoke of the importance of being prepared. He shared how Jack had recently taken him on horseback to the high country fishing, and how the success of the whole trip hinged on his advance preparation. After sharing the Gospel message, he posed the questions "Are you prepared for your final trip which lies ahead?" "Have you done what is required to spend eternity in Heaven?" "Have you accepted Jesus as your personal Savior and Lord?"

Our nephew Lance, sang three of Jack's favorite songs. He was doing an absolutely beautiful job until he began to make eye contact with some family and friends who were sobbing uncontrollably. Swept up in his own emotion over the loss of his beloved Uncle Jack, he totally broke down during his last song. It was hard to watch, but the Maestro knew exactly what He was doing.

He had given the cue to everyone who participated that afternoon, and together they played a beautiful, inspiring song of invitation which rang out loud and clear over the crying and sadness that filled the hearts of all in attendance.

Isaiah 38:1 *"...Put your house in order, because you are going to die...."*

Mission Accomplished

After the service, hundreds of people lined up to come to the front of the church and speak to me. Each one passed by Jack's photo and his personal items, as well as the painting of the horse with no rider. It went on for hours.

One after the next, after the next, they filed by. Each was deeply touched and moved by what they had experienced. One by one they took a moment to tell me how much they loved Jack and how they would never have another friend like him. Many shared something specific with me about a time when Jack reached out to them or helped them. It didn't matter how many people were in line behind them, they had to make their love for Jack known to me.

I always knew how Jack loved his friends and helped people. Their comments made my love for Jack that much stronger and increased the pride I had in being his wife for almost thirty years.

Grown men crying their eyes out approached me to tell me how Jack had taken them thirty miles out in the ocean fishing and while out there he would share his love for God with them.

Others he took on horseback to 11,000 feet elevation, above the tree line, to a place so beautiful it could only have been created by the Hand of God. Jack found such peace and contentment in God's creation, where there were no telephones or anything that would interfere with its beauty and serenity.

I didn't know it until then, but this was how Jack witnessed to his friends. He didn't preach to them, he simply showed them the love of God through creation. As they spoke to me, several expressed they had made a decision, that day, to give their life to the Lord.

For the next two years, I continued to learn of the people whose lives were changed because of Jack's life and tragic death. The Maestro had revealed to me His whole plan as we sat together on the plane in Row 2, Seats A and B.

I could have been singing a mournful lament wallowing in my own grief over the loss of Jack, instead the Maestro was conducting my full orchestra in a song of praise. Many of Jack's friends had been saved! Jack's purpose in life had been fulfilled! Mission accomplished! Praise the Lord! Hallelujah!

John 15:13 *"Greater love has no one than this: that he lay down his life for his friends."*

It Will Sell When It Sells

W hile I stood at the front of the church speaking to each person in the line, I looked up and saw that the next person was our real estate agent and his wife. He hugged me and whispered in my ear, "I have an offer on your place." My response to him was, "This is not a good time, come and see me Monday."

The following day while I was at church and with family, two more offers were made and a bidding war commenced between the buyers driving the price up. This is what Jack and I expected would happen in May when we first listed our home. Jack's words came back to me, "Don't worry; it will sell when it sells."

The following week the bidding came to an end, and our place was sold. I called our accountant, Doyle Blaylock, to give him the news. The Maestro gave the cue to Doyle to reveal to me that I would be receiving the largest financial blessing ever. As soon as I told him our place was sold, he said, "You have got to be the luckiest person I have ever seen in my life." I had no idea what he was talking about, so he went on to explain the IRS law to me.

When you purchase a piece of property, the original purchase price is what the IRS refers to as your "cost basis" in that property. Any money you spend to improve the property while you own it, increases your cost basis. When you sell the property, the difference between the sales price and your cost basis, is your appreciation. Any appreciation over $500,000.00 is heavily taxed by the IRS.

Our cost basis in our property was $10,000.00, what we paid for it in 1974. Over the years we improved the property, putting a lot of money into it, but whatever we needed, we simply brought home from our own lumber yard. Consequently, we had no receipts with which to substantiate the increase in our cost basis to the IRS. So, we would be paying a substantial amount of taxes when the property sold.

Here's the blessing. The IRS law reads that when property is held in Joint Tenancy as ours was, at the time one party dies, the surviving party receives the "step up in cost basis." That meant my cost basis was no longer $10,000.00, but the value of the property on the day of Jack's death.

Had our place sold prior to Jack's death I would have had a huge tax bill with the IRS. The Maestro held up the sale until eight days after his death, giving me the step up in cost basis, and no tax implications. Now that's a blessing! My heart sang out in gratitude for this tremendous gift God had bestowed upon me.

Isaiah 57:14 *"...Remove the obstacles out of the way of my people."*

His Last Visitation

As I stood at the front of the church after Jack's memorial service and talked to each person who spoke to me, I was blessed. Each one had something to say about Jack that deeply touched me. What I learned from the people who approached me that afternoon added to what I already knew about Jack. So many took my hand, and with tears streaming down their face, told me how they loved him, and how he had taken the time for them when they needed it. How he helped them when they needed help. How he stopped to talk when he saw them. How he reached out to them whenever he could. Each one loved him so much and each would miss him deeply. They would never have another friend like Jack Betts.

After Jack made the last trip to California alone, he didn't say much about what he did while he was there. Only that he was busy getting the bulls ready for the long trip back to Oklahoma. At the memorial, I learned he had done far more than just that.

While he was in California those few days, he went out of his way to visit some people. He went to Lodi and bought several lugs of fresh asparagus, packaged it up in zip-lock bags and set out on what would be his last visitation trip. He went to see over twenty people taking them each a package of asparagus and once again sharing his excitement of moving to Oklahoma. As he handed each of them their package he said, "When you fix this asparagus, think of me as I am driving home to Oklahoma."

He also made a special trip to see his sister Betty and take her a lug of peaches. He told her as he was leaving to "Use these peaches however you want, but be sure to make a good cobbler. Wish I could be here to have some with you."

The Maestro had cued Jack to bless all these people one last time. Each one so vividly remembered the last words he said to them. They each commented they knew how busy he was, and yet he took time to visit them. The fact that he stopped by to see them and bring them something meant the world to them now. They never knew it would be the last time they would see his smile as he waved good-bye and drove away.

Jack had blessed them all so much and now their words were blessing me. Through the sadness, somehow joy rang out. The joy I had in knowing how much Jack meant to all these people, and the joy I had for the opportunity of spending so many years of my life as Jack's wife.

Proverbs 27:9 "...*the pleasantness of one's friend springs from his earnest counsel.*"

More From Seat 2B

The following Tuesday I flew back to Dallas, Texas to go home. There was never a doubt in my mind I was supposed to be in Oklahoma, and the Maestro had a plan for the plane trip back.

The trip east was the exact same scenario as the trip west. It was a sold out flight and I had seat 2-A. Seat B was again empty. Or was it? Not hardly. Once again the Maestro took that seat, and in the 2 1/2 hours that followed He shared with me a message that would change the course of my life.

I had lived the last twenty-nine years as "Jack's wife," and I did it proudly. We were a team and did everything together. Jack made the decisions and I stood by them. Together we accomplished a lot, but now everything would be different.

As I sat on the plane in seat 2-A, I heard the voice of the Maestro in my spirit say, "You are no longer Jack's wife. You are my servant, and I have something special for you to do. Something I have been preparing you to do your whole life, and it does not include Jack. I have totally prepared you, and you are still young enough to do it."

I could hardly remember doing anything that didn't include Jack. However, I knew what I was hearing was the voice of God. He had revealed so much to me in the last several days, I recognized His voice. I knew it was Him, and I listened.

On the plane, that day, the Maestro explained to me what His purpose for my life now, was to be. He told me I was to build a retreat facility on my ranch in Oklahoma. This came as quite a shock to me, as I didn't even know what a retreat facility was. I had never been on a retreat. So what did God mean by this? I didn't know. It was what He wanted me to do, and I had to trust Him.

So much had happened in the last thirteen days. The Maestro had conducted my life overture from the full orchestration of joy and abundance in our dream come true, to complete silence in the face of death. His melody revealed His purpose for Jack's life and death and the excitement of the opportunity to participate in an event that would result in souls saved. Now, a whole new outlook on my own life that included a purpose for me alone flowed forth from His score.

Alone. That was the most difficult lyric I had heard in my whole life overture. What a passage of music it was, and I knew in my heart it was far from over. For all these years we planned our lives and now I knew it wasn't our plan at all. It had been the plan of the Maestro all along.

Jeremiah 29:11 *"For I know the plans I have for you," declares the Lord, "plans to prosper you and not to harm you, plans to give you hope and a future."*

A Breathtaking Picture

On the two hour drive home from Dallas to Caney, Oklahoma, I began to sort it all out in my mind. God had revealed to me the purpose of Jack's life, the reason for his death, and now I had been given the assignment to build a retreat facility, and yet I didn't even have a house to live in. First things first, I had to build my home. Jack and I had completed the plans, and I could do this.

I arrived home to my little house in Caney. It was Duncan and me, and once again, I thanked God for the little dog who was my companion. I do not have the words to explain the song of total, overwhelming loneliness that covered me like a heavy blanket as I crawled into bed that night. I had slept alone before, but I knew Jack would be coming home soon, and would wrap his arms around me, pull me to him, hold me tight and tell me he loved me. How I longed to hear his words once again. Those nights were over, and I knew it. I hugged his pillow pretending it was him, knowing in my heart it was not. I could smell his Old Spice after shave which lingered on the pillow case and prayed I would wake up in Jack's arms, and this whole thing would have only been a nightmare; a horrible nightmare.

I cried myself to sleep that night and woke up the next day knowing it was not a nightmare, but a reality. I prayed for strength. I had made it through another night, and now I prayed for the strength to get through another day.

One day at a time, one night at a time. That's the way it would be from now on. At times it would be one moment at a time.

Duncan wanted out, so I opened the door. The warm morning air felt so good I stepped out on the porch. My tear filled eyes followed Duncan as he ran around the house into the yard. At that moment, with a wave of the baton, the Maestro, the Almighty Painter, created for me a picture that was breathtaking. It was the picture of the beautiful Oklahoma morning sky.

I grabbed Duncan, threw him in the truck, and headed to the big oak tree on the hill. I got out and sat where Jack and I had sat together those mornings just two weeks ago. So much had happened since then. In a way, it seemed like an eternity had passed. As I sat alone in our special place, I felt Jack's presence. Then I heard the Maestro sing His own song to me in my spirit, "I have many more beautiful mornings to show you. I am with you and I will give you the strength you need. Follow me."

Psalm 30:5 *"...weeping may remain at night, but rejoicing comes in the morning."*

Back to Work

I put Duncan back in the truck and went back to the little house. My work ethic kicked into gear. I had a house to build and lot to do. That's what Jack would want me to do, and that's exactly what I was going to do. Build our home.

I walked in the house, picked up the phone, and called Dusty. There was no time for small talk, I had work to do. As soon as he answered his phone, I said, "This is Doreen, do you still want to help me build my house?"

Sheepishly he asked, "Are you still going to build it?"

"Of course I am." I answered, "Are you going to help me?"

"I'll be right there." he said and hung up.

I had learned a lot from Jack about building over the past twenty-nine years. I knew what had to be done and the order in which to do it. I could do this. With a little help, I could build this house.

Strength, that's what I needed, emotional strength. I had the physical strength, but it was emotional strength I was lacking. I prayed, "Please God, give me strength. The strength I need to do this." At that moment the Maestro gave the cue to my memory. Philippians 4:13 *"I can do everything through Him who gives me strength."* He would provide the strength; I knew He would.

I recalled what I had learned from Jack, "The first thing to do on any building project is to prepare the site and bring in the utilities." The site was established and the water was already there. Jack and I had met with a local man about putting in a new septic system, so the only thing left was the electricity. I reached for the phone and dialed the electric company. The engineer answered and I told him to go ahead with the plans he and I had discussed for a larger electric service for my new home. He said the work could be done that week, and we would have temporary power while we were under construction. The project was underway.

I pulled myself together and put on some work clothes. Dusty would be there any minute. I had to be strong and move forward with my life. Once again I must play the theme song of work Jack and I had played together for so long, but now I would be playing by myself.

Philippians 4:13 "*I can do everything through Him who gives me strength.*"

A Memory

Within minutes Dusty pulled up in front of the little house. Ready to go to work, I stepped out on the porch to meet him. The passenger door opened and Dusty's daughter, Faith, slid out. I learned later that his niece Hope, had gone home to Iowa.

Faith ran straight for me. She climbed the stairs, threw her tiny arms around me and hugged me tight for a long while. I hugged her back. Finally she pushed away looked up at me with those big blue eyes and said, "I'm so sorry to hear about Jack, he was the nicest man I ever met."

So much for my emotional strength. I just pulled her to me, and as I held her in my arms, I realized what had happened. The Maestro had given this beautiful little girl the cue to bless me with a very special gift; the gift of a wonderful memory.

Just two weeks prior, Jack came home for lunch and sat down at our little kitchen table and talked with Faith and Hope. The way he responded to the girls that day was totally out of character for him. I remember being in complete shock over his response to those two little, giggling girls who sat playing at the table where he would want to sit and eat his lunch. His response was not at all what I expected it to be. Puzzled, I thought, "Who is this person in Jack's sweaty clothes?"

Two days later, Jack was gone. I had a lot of memories of Jack with children, and most of them were not good. That day, two days before he died, the Maestro gave Jack the cue to be a blessing to Faith and Hope. This is the last memory I have of Jack with a child, and I know God worked through him that day to create this memory just for me.

It is a wonderful memory, one I shall never forget, and as I stood on the porch that day holding little Faith close to me, my heart sang the song of thankfulness to God who is the creator of all things. All things, even memories.

Ecclesiastes 11:5 *"...you cannot understand the work of God, the Maker of all things."*

Prayer Meeting

That very night I went to church for our regular Wednesday night pot luck supper and prayer meeting. As I sat there in the fellowship hall of Ward's Chapel, I knew this was the first of many times I would be there without Jack. Ward's Chapel was his home church, now I felt like it was mine as well.

Our plan of being a part of Ward's Chapel together was not God's plan. I was to be a part of Ward's Chapel without Jack. How could I do that? Jack had always been the spiritual leader of our family; how could I do this alone? How could I sit in a pew at his home church without his arm around my shoulder or his hand in mine? How could I have fellowship with this wonderful church family that consisted of so many of Jack's biological family members without him? How could I sing my part without him singing bass next to me?

The Maestro was filling me with one song after another, each ending up in the air somewhere with a question mark for which I had no answer. I never asked God, "Why?" I only asked Him, "How?" How was I going to do this? He had told me the answer to, "Why?" Now I needed the answer to, "How?"

That's when the Maestro whispered in my ear, "Tell them what I have done for you. Tell them what has happened."

I got up, walked to the table where Pastor Tom was seated, and asked him if I could speak to the church family after supper. He agreed. I had not prepared any remarks; I had no notes. I just allowed God to speak through me to my friends and family at Ward's Chapel. I told them what God had revealed to me about the purpose of Jack's life, and the reason for his tragic death. I shared with them what happened at his memorial service in California; how so many of his friends were saved that day. Then I shared with them God's purpose for my life now, which included being a part of Ward's Chapel without Jack. It also included developing a retreat facility on my ranch in Caney.

They just sat there and listened that night. Their eyes filled with tears at times, and I could see the look of wonderment in their eyes as they listened to what God was saying through me. When I finished speaking the Maestro put a song in my heart I had never sung before. It was a combination of many familiar tunes all played at the same time: Grief and loneliness played right over the top of joy, fulfillment, determination, gratitude, and anticipation. What a song. What a Maestro!

Psalm 40:10 "*I do not hide your righteousness in my heart; I speak of your faithfulness and your salvation....*"

Jack's Clothes

My home in California had sold, which meant another trip west to move my household belongings to Oklahoma. Our church family and friends turned out in droves to help load the truck which I would drive back to Oklahoma. God had prepared me for this task as well. I had driven many trucks over the years.

Finally, I had everything I owned in Oklahoma, and had it all stored or put away with the exception of one thing, Jack's clothes. What would I do with all of Jack's clothes? Jack took such pride in his appearance. He liked clothes, and he had a lot of them. Good clothes, really good clothes. Not the kind you drop of at the Thrift Store donation station. These clothes needed to be used by someone who would appreciate them. That's what Jack would want, and I had a huge pile of very good, expensive clothes.

I called Pastor Tom and asked if he knew of anyone who could use some good clothes. He couldn't think of anyone right off hand, but volunteered to come over and pick them up, just to ease this burden on me. As Tom drove away with Jack's clothes piled in his truck, it was one more piece of Jack that was gone. I would never again be able to help him button his sleeve, straighten his tie, or give him a big hug after smoothing a wrinkle out of his shirt. His clothes were gone, and so was he. I fell on the bed where his clothes had been and sobbed. "I should have kept something, something to hold, something to remember him by."

The next day Pastor Tom called and asked me if it would bother me if I saw someone wearing Jack's clothes. My immediate response was, "No. I would love for someone to be able to use them." The following Sunday when I arrived at Ward's Chapel I couldn't help but notice that Pastor Tom was wearing one of Jack's shirts. As I looked further, I saw that everything he was wearing had belonged to Jack.

After the service Tom approached me and asked if he could speak to me. With his eyes filled with tears he explained that for their whole adult life his wife, Jeri, had been going to school and they had lived only on a pastor's salary. They had three children to feed and clothe, and it seemed as though he came last in line for clothes.

Then the Maestro gave my Pastor, Tom Hargrave, the cue to speak a blessing to me and he said, "I have never in my adult life had clothes in my closet to choose from. All of Jack's clothes fit me perfectly and I never thought I would ever own clothes as nice as these."

I hugged Jack's shirt which was on Tom's body, and my heart overflowed with joy as every musician played a wonderful melody of rejoicing praise to God for what He had done. Jack may not be at Ward's Chapel, but his clothes would be, worn by the pastor he longed to know.

Nehemiah 12:43 "...*rejoicing because God had given them great joy.*"

My Husband

Each morning I prayed for strength to get through that day, whatever that day may bring with it. God had given me a plan and a purpose, so I needed to get on with it and get back to work. The song of work that Jack and I played so perfectly together would now be mine alone to play, but I would play it with every ounce of breath that God gave me. I knew how to work, so once again, my life overture would play my middle ground theme song of work and productivity.

Every day became a little easier than the one before. God was supplying the strength He had promised, and my home was well underway. Each night as I lay in bed I held tight to Jack's pillow. The scent of his Old Spice became more faint with each passing night. Through my tears I prayed to God, thanking Him for what had been accomplished that day. He blessed me with the ability to rest and sleep.

I arose each morning, prayed, and did my Bible reading as my preparation for what would come my way that day. God's Word spoke to me in ways I never knew before. I would read a passage I had read a hundred times before. Now it took on a whole new meaning.

I missed Jack so much. His knowledge of building, his ability to talk to people, and his strong back. I should have learned more when I had the chance. I needed him so much to help me build our dream home. Who would be there for me now? Who would know the answers to all these questions? Who would I rely on for help; for their expertise? Who could I trust? Who would be there to encourage me? No one could ever fill the void I had in my life that was once filled by my husband, Jack.

One morning about a month later, the Maestro spoke through His Word. The night before at church, Richard Betts had shared with us how he told someone to just open their bible and start reading. It didn't matter where, just open it and God's word would speak to their heart.

Remembering what Richard had said, the next morning I picked up my Bible and opened it somewhere in the middle. I looked down at the page, and there it was! My eyes went straight to it as if it were printed in bold print. Isaiah 54:4-5 *"Remember no more the reproach of your widowhood. For your Maker is your husband— the Lord Almighty is his name."*

Richard was right! I wasn't without a husband; my Maker is my husband! There it was, right there in black and white. I had read Isaiah many times and had never seen that passage before. It was as if God saved this scripture until I needed it; I needed it now. Again I sang the song of praise to my Lord, my Savior, my Husband.

Proverbs 2:1-5 *"...if you accept my words...then you will understand...and find the knowledge of God."*

Second Verse

O ne Sunday morning while studying my lesson for Sunday School, wanting to make some notes, I opened my desk drawer and reached for a pad of paper. What I thought was just another yellow pad, was actually the same pad I had with me when my dog, Duncan, and I made that long, hard trip from California in May. We were moving our little ranch pick up, which had no air conditioning or radio, to Oklahoma. Instantly I remembered the trip and the words God gave me as I drove across the desert.

There written on the pad were the lyrics of the parody to the old Patsy Cline song, "I Cry Myself to Sleep Each Night." I recalled longing for more words to come, but they just wouldn't. I hadn't looked at it, or thought about it since, but now it was once again before me. I put the pad down on my desk and began getting ready for church.

As I stood in the hot shower I sang the little song as if I had just written the words that morning, but this time the rest of the words came. They came as easily as the first ones came when I drove the truck months earlier. God had given me the first verse then, but now He had more, and the time had come for me to know the rest.

I pray myself to sleep each night, the Lord's Prayer I first recite,
Then I thank the Lord for blessing me.

I list the things I'm grateful for, every night there's something more,
Everything I have, He gave to me.

1st Verse
Good friends, my church, my family, these I'm grateful for,
My health, His guidance, and His Word; Oh there's so much more.

And so each night before I sleep, I thank the Lord for blessing me,
Everything I have, He gave to me.

2nd Verse
The strength to face another day, my peace and joy within,
His unconditional grace and love, eternal life with Him.

And so each night before I sleep, I thank the Lord for blessing me,
Everything I have, He gave to me....Everything I am, He gave to me.

He waited to give me the second verse until that morning. I had so much more to be grateful for. The strength to face another day, peace, joy, unconditional grace and love, and most importantly, eternal life with Him. Everything I have, and everything I am, He gave to me.

I had cried myself to sleep each night since Jack died. It was time I prayed myself to sleep with a grateful heart for everything I had, and everything I am; knowing it all comes from Him.

2 Peter 1:3 *"His divine power has given us everything we need for life...."*

Life Purpose Scripture

One evening in late September I received a telephone call from a friend in California. The purpose of the call was to inform me that the Elk Grove Rotary Club (where Jack was an active member) had decided to dedicate their annual fund raiser to Jack. This event was a Formal Charity Ball held each October, and they were hoping I would be able to attend.

This would mean another trip to California, but I felt so blessed, and honored, by their decision to dedicate this community event to Jack, I agreed to go. I made my plane reservations and arranged to stay the first two nights with my good friends Gary and Paralee Wright. Gary was a member of Rotary Club and I could attend this special event with them. It was not easy going to this function without Jack, but it was something I needed to do. The event went very well, and was a tremendous financial success as it was every year.

Since Jack's sister, Betty, lives in the area, I stayed the next two nights with her where I was able to visit with some of the family at a dinner party she hosted. When I went to bed that evening I was feeling very lonely. I missed Jack so much. I opened my Bible to do some reading and turned to Philippians. As I began to read in chapter one, I could relate to the writer, Paul. He was in prison when he wrote this letter to the Philippians, and spoke of being in chains. He realized his strength, and ability to endure imprisonment, came from his faith in Jesus Christ. As I continued to read I realized, like Paul, I was in chains; chains of grief and despair. It was so hard doing everything I had to do without Jack. At times the weight of these chains seemed almost unbearable.

In verse twenty Paul writes that it would be much easier to die then to go on like this. He knew God had work for him to do, but to die would be more desirable, since he knew upon his death he would be with Christ. Should he continue with his struggle to spread the Gospel in any way he could, or should he take the easy way out and die? Then Paul wrote in Philippians 1:22-26 *"Yet what shall I choose? I do not know! I am torn between the two: I desire to depart and be with Christ, which is better by far; but it is more necessary for you that I remain in the body. Convinced of this, I know that I will remain, and I will continue with all of you for your progress and joy in the faith, so that through my being with you again your joy in Christ Jesus will overflow on account of me."*

After reading this I sat up in bed and read it again. I felt like Paul had written this specifically for me. I knew God had a plan and a purpose for the rest of my life, but this scripture brought it all into prospective. We do not live for ourselves, but for the spiritual progress of those God puts within our reach. I got a pen and underlined these verses in my Bible, and I wrote in the margin next to them, "My purpose for living." This passage has become my "Life Purpose" scripture.

That night God played a beautiful violin solo in my life overture. The sweet, fluent melody, to the lyrics of my Life Purpose scripture penetrated my heart and have resonated there ever since.

Philippians 1:26 *"through my being with you...your joy in Christ Jesus will overflow on account of me."*

Too Soon

The construction of my home was coming along nicely; I was coming to grips with my life. Wednesday evening, December 10, 2003, when I returned home form church, the phone rang. It was my daughter, Michelle. Her water had broken and they were transporting her to Spokane, Washington where her baby boy would be born. I made flight reservations and left the following morning from Dallas and flew to Spokane. I went to the hospital and although Michelle had not yet delivered, she and her unborn baby were hooked up to machines and monitors.

It was far too soon for this child to be born after all he was not scheduled to arrive until late February. I prayed for this little child as we all knew he was a miracle. How small would he be? Would he be born alive? Would the doctors be able to save him? What kind of problems would he have? What would happen in the days, months, and years that lie ahead? So many questions and no answers.

I tried to stay focused on the fact God had a plan and this tiny child was a part of it. This miracle baby, who, according to the doctors, was never supposed to be conceived, was alive and well in Michelle's womb. We had to have faith that he would be born healthy.

The doctors tried their best to keep him in the womb for as long as possible so his tiny lungs, organs, and brain could develop. On Sunday, December 14, 2003 this little boy was ready to be born, and the doctors weren't stopping him. Michelle's husband, Matt, went in the delivery room with her while I stayed with his parents in the waiting room. The doctors said she would probably be having an emergency C-Section, so we were prepared for the worst. It wasn't long until Matt emerged from the delivery room and said the baby had been born naturally and appeared fine. Our hearts sang the grateful song of praise for this child who had beat the odds.

Then a doctor came out and said abruptly, "Michelle had a rough time of it. We are running some tests on the baby and will keep you posted." With that he turned and disappeared through the giant doors. What did he mean? Was the baby okay? What were they testing him for? How was Michelle? Again we prayed.

Approximately an hour later another doctor emerged and said, "Michelle is fine. The baby is fine. He weighs 4 pounds 6 ounces, and is 16 inches long. His lungs are fully developed and he is breathing completely on his own. As far as we can tell, he's perfect."

My song of sadness and grief turned to happiness and joy with the birth of a grandson. God had taken Jack but sent a baby boy. He was breathing and perfect.

Job 33:4 *"The Spirit of God has made me; the breath of the Almighty gives me life."*

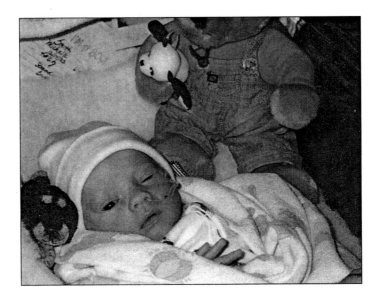

Baby Joseph

Joseph Hayes Smith

Michelle and Matt named the baby Joseph Hayes Smith. He had Jack's middle name, Hayes. What a legacy Jack had left for this little boy who would never know him.

The doctors said Joseph would probably be staying in the hospital until his original due date, which was late in February, but we were all determined to bring him home long before that. We worked with him day and night and he progressed well. The doctors had certain criteria he had to meet before they would release him. We knew what they required and we were determined to have him meet all criteria as soon as possible.

January 1, 2004, New Year's Day, Michelle and Matt took little Joseph Hayes Smith home to Moscow, Idaho where Matt was in school finishing his master's degree. It had only been eighteen days since his birth and he was ready to go home. He passed all the tests and they released him. He was a fighter from the day he was born.

I followed them home and was prepared to stay until I felt sure Michelle was strong enough to take care of little Joseph. They both did well, and I only stayed four more days. It was hard to leave them, but I had a construction project in Oklahoma to get back to. I knew they would be just fine.

While on the plane to Dallas, I took out the photos of my precious little grandson, Joseph. My life overture took on a new song. The Maestro had given the cue to this little, tiny baby who would be the next musician in my orchestra. At less than a month old, this tiny musician was already playing a song of courage, strength, and determination.

As I sat on the plane looking at his photographs, the Maestro revealed to me an additional blessing He had bestowed.

Christmas was a special time of year for our family. Jack and I enjoyed it very much. I remembered dreading what Christmas would be like without Jack. Yes, there was family in Oklahoma, but Michelle was in Idaho and Jack was gone. No matter how hard I tried, it would be a horrible time and I knew it. But, God had another plan. Not only did He send me a beautiful, perfect grandson to love and cherish, but he brought him into this world on December 14th, which meant I would not have to spend my first Christmas without Jack alone. As we celebrated the greatest gift ever given, the miracle birth of the Son of God, I also celebrated the gift of a grandson, who was also a miracle.

Psalm 30:11 *"You turned my wailing into dancing..."*

Welcome Home

I had spoken with Matt and Michelle about the possibility of them living in Oklahoma after Matt graduated. They could choose a home site and live here on the ranch. Michelle didn't seem interested at the time because her memories of the hot summer weather were more than she could bear.

You can imagine my surprise when I received a call in February; they had discussed it and decided to "take me up on my offer." My house was almost finished and I would soon be moving in. I was excited about their upcoming visit during Matt's Spring Break from school in March.

They looked great and little Joseph had grown a lot since I last saw him in January. I watched Joseph while Michelle and Matt searched the ranch for what would be the perfect site for their home. By the end of the week all the plans had been made. They chose a spot about 1/2 mile from my house. Next they went to Ada, Oklahoma and settled on a very nice modular home which would be delivered in June. They would be moving here soon after Matt's graduation.

My overture took on a whole new feel. My daughter and her family would be here soon and excitement filled every measure my orchestra played. I would not be here alone! To have Michelle, Matt, and little Joseph right here on the ranch was something I never expected. I would be able to watch Joseph grow and develop from a baby, to a toddler, to a little boy, and then into a fine young man. He would be big and strong with a heart for God, and a wonderful addition to my orchestra.

These new plans meant another home site to prepare and more work. The utilities had to be brought to the site and a road built to access it. My theme song of work fired up one more time. I was off and running on another building project.

Every musician was in tune and playing well. It sounded good but I could detect a flaw. There was an absence in the overall sound like a big hole in the bottom. Everyone was trying their best to play, but it was obvious something was missing. There was no strength in the bass section and it was apparent Jack was not there to play. We would have to pick up the slack, play louder, and try to play his part. It would not be easy.

The Maestro cued me to begin playing my song of determination and the lyrics came into my head, "When the going gets tough, the tough get going." I would have to get tough and learn to play Jack's part. I knew I could never play it like he did, but with God's help I could hold my own on bass.

Nahum 1:7 *"The Lord is good, a refuge in times of trouble...."*

Keep Praying

I had moved into my new home and the preparation for Matt and Michelle's home site was taking shape. It was late spring and I was having the landscaping done at my house. So much had transpired in the last ten months.

I woke up one Sunday morning with a start, and a horrible realization. Between building my home, going to Spokane for Joseph's birth, and getting the home site ready for Matt and Michelle, I had completely forgotten about our cattle. I had not even looked at them for months.

As I lay in bed that morning I knew the cows were going to start calving and I didn't have any help. I was afraid a lot of the young cows would have to have their calves pulled, and I was alone. I had helped Jack with the cows over the years, but I would not be able to do this by myself. All my cows were going to start calving and what was I going to do?

I got dressed and went to church where I prayed through the whole service. I was worried sick over my cows. They had probably started to calve already and some of them could be dead. The harder I prayed, the more I worried. After church I spoke to Pastor Tom about it and he told me to keep praying and God would send me the answer.

I went home and prayed all afternoon for an answer on my cows. I thought about driving to the back side of the ranch to see how many had already calved or died, but I didn't have the heart to look.

I went back to church that night and prayed through another service. After church my pastor asked me if I had received the answer to my dilemma. When I told him "No" he simply said, "Keep praying, God will send you the answer."

I was up half the night praying and worrying about the cows. What was I going to do? As I continued to pray I could hear the moaning sound of off-key violas and cellos. They sounded like dying cattle drowning out my praying, pleading, and worrying.

When I got up the next morning, I had worried my self sick over the cows and I felt horrible. I could hear Pastor Tom's words in my head, "Keep praying, God will send you the answer."

Psalm 4:1 "*...God, give me relief from my distress; be merciful to me and hear my prayer.*"

Help!

I was totally exhausted and feeling terrible. About 8:30 AM someone knocked on my kitchen door. Thinking it was one of the landscaping crew, I answered the knock. Standing at my door was my neighbor, Brad Lahman, whose ranch adjoins mine on the southeast side. I recognized him, because he and his wife attended Jack's funeral. Brad was a tall, young cowboy with a big, strong, bass voice. He looked down into my tired, red eyes, and in a very serious way said, "I need to talk to you." I looked up at him and thought, "Now what? Lord, I can't take much more." I asked him to come in and have a cup of coffee, to which he responded, "Don't want no coffee, but I need to talk to you……….now." He came in and sat down at my kitchen counter. After a long pause, he proceeded to tell me what happened to him the day before. His story did not come easily because he didn't know how I would receive what he was about to tell me.

He began by saying that his wife made him come and talk to me. He asked if I knew that his house overlooked my ranch, to which I responded, "Yes, I know where you live." He was really beating around the bush, and I was beginning to think he was a little crazy, when he said, "I don't want you to think I'm buttin' into your business, because I don't butt into anyone's business, but,"……… "Yesterday morning, about 11:30, my wife and I were sitting at our kitchen table having a cup of coffee. As we sat there looking out the window over the ranch, all of a sudden, an overwhelming feeling came over me that you may need some help with your cows."

I couldn't believe my ears. He was a direct answer to my prayer. God had sent the help I'd been praying for. I told Brad that I had been praying the last twenty-four hours for help. After we both shed some tears, we worked out an arrangement whereby Brad would completely take care of my cattle. I didn't know Brad at all, but I knew God sent him, and that's all I needed to know.

Brad received the message from God while sitting at his kitchen table at 11:30 Sunday morning, which was the exact time I was sitting in church praying my heart out for an answer. I prayed all afternoon and all night making myself sick, but God heard me the first time. He heard my cry for help and answered my prayer.

With a wave of the baton, the Maestro covered Brad with an overwhelming feeling that was so strong, he knew he had to respond. The moaning of the cellos replicating dying cows, ceased as every musician in my orchestra played another wonderful song of praise, and now Brad would be playing bass in all the songs about cowboys and cattle.

Isaiah 30:19 *"...How gracious He will be when you cry for help! As soon as He hears, He will answer you."*

A Look Back

O ne day while having lunch with some friends, one of the ladies asked me, "You are so strong. Where do you get your strength?"

I had never given it much thought until that moment. As I sat there pondering my answer, God spoke to my spirit and said, "Look back over your life. Can you see them? Can you see who was there for you?"

At that moment, with a wave of the baton, the Maestro gave the cue to several musicians who had long ago each played their song in my life overture. I immediately recognized each person's style and melody. I hadn't heard them for a long time but there they were, in the forefront of my mind, playing their hearts out on their favorite tune. With their repeat performance came the revelation of the blessing. God had brought these people into my life to prepare me for where I was now. One by one I heard their song and could picture each one and the part they played in shaping my life.

As I described them to my friends, it became apparent that they all had something in common. They were all women who were alone, and all but one had become widows at a young age. They were strong and industrious women who never felt sorry for themselves, or spoke of their need for another husband. They had learned to take care of themselves and find contentment where they were. They were all different, and yet they all had this one commonality.

Over the next several days I searched my past for other people who stood out as those I looked up to and admired - those who taught me the important lessons of life. I looked in old photo albums in search of those people who played a large part in molding my character.

Other than Jack, who taught me so much, it was these women. It was their songs that played out loud and clear. It was the lyrics of their melodies that I could recall so quickly and vividly. Each song was a familiar refrain that I had adapted to fit my own life overture. I was playing their tunes, and I had been for a long time. I was now playing as I had watched them play, as a widow.

Philippians 4:11"...*I have learned to be content whatever the circumstances."*

The Women

These are the women and the songs they played in my life overture.

My Grandmother. Grandma taught me determination, independence, persistence, fortitude, to work hard, and not be afraid to get my hands dirty or blistered. She encouraged me and told me I could do anything, I just had to learn how. She drove the first nails in what would build my self-confidence.

My Aunt Emma. She taught me love for the piano, and the joy it could bring.

My Aunt Alice. She shared with me her gift of hospitality, and taught me how to be social, love people, and have fun, all at the same time. She also taught me to read my Bible every day, and to do my best to live by its teachings.

My Aunt Lil. She taught me ingenuity and the love of the domestic side of life. From her I learned to make the best use of everything, not wasting anything. I learned to not only belong, but to do my part. She taught me to be organized and that everything has its place. She also sparked my interest in current, and world affairs, and to be involved in my community.

Mrs. Halsey. She taught me that the piano is my friend. I learned that I could sit down, and as I began to play, I could be transformed, bringing me out of depression or heartbreak. I learned to play myself away from that dark place and into the light. I was able to get lost in the music as I allowed it to speak to me. I could make every song my own, and take from the music whatever it was I needed.

My mother-in-law, Ruby Betts. From Ruby I learned to have faith. She taught me not to worry about anything, but simply put all my trust in God for everything. I learned what it meant to be a devoted Christian and member of a church family. She taught me to read and study the Bible and that the answers to all my life questions were written in this holy book.

God brought me into the presence of all these wonderful women throughout my life, and each would play a part in preparing me for my life as a young widow. All of them taught me, not by telling me, but by the example they lived everyday.

These women are all gone, but their songs live on as I do my best to mirror their melodies in my life overture.

1 John 3:18 *"Dear children, let us not love with words or tongue, but with actions and in truth."*

Estelle

Since I have lived in Oklahoma, the Maestro has given the cue to yet another strong, wonderful woman who has played a wonderful melody in my life overture. This woman, like the others, was widowed at a young age. Her name is Estelle Hinson. She is one of Jack's many cousins, and is a combination of several of the other mentors that have meant so much to me throughout my life.

Estelle is strong, independent, and resourceful. She is a hard worker and always does her part at church or wherever she is involved. She is not afraid to get her hands dirty or blistered, and willingly jumps into a project with both feet. In addition to all this, she is a woman of tremendous faith and a fierce prayer warrior who never gives up. Estelle lives every day to glorify God, and her life has been a tremendous example for me.

From the first day I met her, Estelle has been a blessing. She is a wealth of knowledge, and although she lives by faith, she is able to have a realistic view of things as well. She has played a wonderful song of encouragement and hope, and never fails to listen, pray, and give her opinion when asked.

She is twenty-five years older than I and fills a void that I have felt my whole life. She is like the mother I never really had. I am grateful for her love, acceptance, encouragement, and participation in my life. Most of all I am grateful for her prayer life which includes me every day.

Estelle understands me and I understand her. Our life overtures have played many of the same tunes over the years, parallel melodies being played simultaneously by two different musicians. She adds a vignette to my life overture like none other at this time, and I pray God gives her many more years to play.

I know that God is providing for my every need as I attempt to live for Him as a widow, in a world of couples.

He has provided role model after role model to set the example for me. The Maestro continues to direct Estelle, as she plays her faithful song of prayer, love, encouragement and strength, without skipping a beat.

2 Timothy 1:3 *"...night and day I constantly remember you in my prayers."*

Estelle

Never Alone

While on a road trip with some friends, I was asked, "How do you deal with being alone?" I thought about it for minute, and responded, "I try to stay busy, but I don't really feel like I'm alone."

At that moment, a bright light came on in my head, and the Maestro gave me the revelation of a huge blessing He had bestowed on me a few years earlier. Suddenly it was all very clear what had happened. In 1999, He gave me the gift of a musical play called "Never Alone." Then in the spring of 2003 my pastor in California insisted we do a repeat performance of it before Jack and I moved to Oklahoma. It wasn't easy, but we did it.

The premise of the play is that no matter how bad things get, whoever may betray you, hurt you, leave you, or die, you are never alone. No matter what happens, if you have faith in God, you are "Never Alone." The play was a blessing to all who saw it both times, but what I came to know at that moment, was that it was as much for me as it was for the others. God had given me a gift that would speak more to me than anyone who witnessed it.

It was a project I simply could not stop working on until it was completed and first brought to the stage in 2000. Then in 2003 my pastor in California insisted we do it again. Why would he do that? It hadn't been that long since we did it the first time. This revelation brought the answer. God wanted the message to be fresh in my mind. He wanted me to know what I was trying to impart to others; the message that even though Jack was gone, I would never be alone.

This revelation was amazing! God knew what I would be facing, and He knew I needed to know that He would never leave me alone. He gave me the message in the form of this musical play, and then showed me a rerun performance just three months before Jack died.

As we drove that afternoon the Maestro cued every musician in my orchestra to play all the songs He had given me for the play, but now it was clear why I had been given them. What a revelation! What a gift! What a blessing! The blessing of knowing, no matter what, I am never alone.

Hebrews 13:5 ...*God has said, "Never will I leave you; never will I forsake you."*

Garage Addition

In November 2006, it had been over two years since I built anything, and it was high time the builder's song be heard again in my overture. I was on the Building Committee at Ward's Chapel, and involved with the new auditorium we were building, but it wasn't the same as being "hands on" working on a project. I was anxious to sing my favorite tune "Slivers and Blisters," one more time.

I was out in my garage one day and I came to the conclusion it simply wasn't big enough. It was 28 feet by 28 feet, but it needed to be 20 feet longer. I surveyed the area and found it to be a feasible plan and not that difficult. A garage addition would be my next building project, but I needed someone to help me. My previous helpers had moved away, but the Maestro had prepared just the right person, and he was ready and waiting in the wings.

Jack's cousin, Beverly and her husband Scott had recently dissolved their business which required Scott to frequently work out of town. They had two sons who were getting older and needed their dad at home more where he could take part in their activities. Scott, being a very good builder and having worked in the trades his whole life, started a business doing handyman work and small remodel jobs in the area, so I contacted him about my project.

Scott and I quickly came to an agreement and went right to work on the garage addition. Working with Scott was much like working with Jack. He was knowledgeable, reliable, even tempered, and we had mutual respect for each other's abilities. This made him very easy to work along side, and together we played a harmonious duet of hard work and productivity, to which we sang the familiar lyrics, "slivers, blisters, and sore muscles."

The project went well, but because of the holidays and inclement weather, it took a bit longer than we anticipated. However, by early January it neared completion. Scott would be arriving at 8:00 AM and we would put the plate covers on the outlets and the other few remaining finishing touches. Another building project was on the verge of completion, and I was excited about being able to once again play the happy refrain of accomplishment.

2 Corinthians 8:11 *"Now finish the work, so that your eager willingness to do it may be matched by your completion of it..."*

Year of Jubilee

Through the building of my home, guest house, landscaping, Michelle and Matt's home, and now the garage addition, God kept tapping me on the shoulder and whispering in my ear a tune that was becoming very familiar. It went something like this: *"Don't forget about the project I have for you. Remember, I want you to build a retreat facility on the ranch."*

I had been giving it a lot of thought and formulating in my mind what it should be like, but now God really began to put the pressure on me to stop thinking and start doing. His song changed from a soft, whisper of a sweet violin playing, *"Don't forget about me,"* to the riveting trumpets playing loud and clear, *"Get me off the back burner."*

The morning of the final day on the garage addition, I woke up at 3:00 AM and could not go back to sleep. I turned on the television in my room, which was on one of the Christian Network channels. A young, dynamic woman preacher was speaking on a subject I had never heard before: The Year of Jubilee. She sparked my attention and I listened as she explained that every seven years God brings things to completion. This was January, 2007, and was the beginning of the seventh year, making 2007 the Year of Jubilee.

After bringing credence to her sermon with plenty of scripture references she brought her forceful message to a close by pointing her index finger at me, I mean at the camera, and saying, "And so, if God has been telling you to do something, this is the year to do it."

I had heard enough of her demanding tone, so I grabbed the remote and promptly turned her, and the television, off.

I got out of bed, went into my sewing room where I have a large counter space, got out two pieces of white poster board, my builders scale, a sharp pencil, and began drawing plans.

Before Scott arrived for work at 8:00 AM I had two complete sets of house plans drawn. Another project was in the making, only this time it was God's project. He was off the back burner, and the fire was turned up. Let the music begin, one more time!

Luke 11:28 *"Blessed...are those who hear the word of God and obey it."*

One More Time

At 8:00 AM I was waiting in the garage when Scott arrived. We did the few things that were needed to finish up the project and after loading up his tools, Scott said, "Well, I guess this wraps up this job."

In response I said, "Yeah, how would you like to build a house?"

"A whole house?" He asked.

"Yep, and kind of a big one. Wait right here, I'll be right back." With that, I ran in the house, got the two sets of plans I had drawn earlier in the morning, and dashed back to the garage. I unrolled them and spread them out on the counter.

"You can pick it." I said, "I'm going to build one of these houses, and you can choose."

Scott looked at me and said, "You're serious, aren't you?"

"Very serious, and if you don't want to help me I will find someone who does."

Scott carefully examined both sets of plans. After making his choice, he pointed to one and said, "I like this one."

"I do too." I answered and with that I tore the other one up and threw it in the garbage can. Then I asked, "When can you start?"

The house would be a 4,000 square foot, rustic log cabin with 5 bedrooms, 7 bathrooms, and a large upstairs multipurpose room. I calculated it would take 6 to 9 months to build depending on the weather, and availability of material.

Scott explained he was committed to another job which would take about four months. So, while he was doing that I would do the site work; level and compact the ground, bring in the electricity and water, and have the septic system installed.

The project was underway, and the Maestro had just given the cue to the man I needed to help me build it. I was flying high and my whole orchestra was in full swing and singing "happy days are here again, let the song of work begin again." I think even the Maestro may have been dancing Himself as He conducted this one.

Proverbs 19:21 *"Many are the plans in a man's heart, but it is the Lord's purpose that prevails."*

Fishing and Feathers

All wives deal with certain idiosyncrasies, or habits, their husbands possess, and I was no exception. Jack's favorite pastime, when he wasn't working, was to fish, and he also took pleasure in collecting feathers.

Jack would go fishing every chance he could. He found peace and serenity while sitting on a rock which formed part of the border of a mountain lake, far from civilization, alone in God's beautiful creation. Also, he enjoyed being twenty or thirty miles out in the ocean where no land was in sight in any direction on the horizon. The solitude of such places brought him peace and renewal.

In the last ten years of his life, he was involved in off-shore game fishing and entered several tournaments. He really liked this because it was a combination of hunting and fishing, both of which were exciting to him.

One of his favorite places to fish was Alaska. The fishing was great and the beauty of the environment left him speechless. On one such fishing expedition, he shared with me how one day he just sat in the boat and watched the eagles all day; a pair of adolescent male eagles practicing diving for prey, then flying straight up in the air as fast as they could. Sometimes they would free fall, head over heels, and pull out of the fall moments before hitting the rocks. As he sat quietly in the boat, he watched as they performed their antics then effortlessly soared in huge circles over his head.

From that trip he brought home a perfect young eagle feather that had been shed by one of the birds. It was absolutely beautiful, without blemish, and was one of his prize positions. Jack loved that feather and displayed it proudly at the lumber yard for several years.

When a customer would ask about it, he would carefully take it down and describe the time he forfeited a day of fishing to just sit in the boat and watch one of the most beautiful birds in all of God's creation.

I never asked him about his love for feathers it was just something I lived with over the years. Wherever Jack went he seemed to find a perfect feather. He would often come home with a gorgeous specimen from a golden pheasant that he would keep in his truck or a tiny, fuzzy feather from a baby sparrow that he would put in his hat band.

Once, when asked about the feather in his hat he said, "It helps me to fly straight."

Psalm 91:4 *"He will cover you with his feathers, and under his wings you will find refuge..."*

Stopped In My Tracks

The spring of 2007 brought a lot of rain which put Scott and I a little behind schedule on our building project. However, by the first of July we were well into the framing process. By mid August we had the ground floor framed and had completely sheeted the exterior with plywood. The roof truss package had been set on the plate line.

Scott and I rolled and stood all the trusses in one day, which were engineered to be 16 inches on center apart. They had to be close together to carry the load of the upstairs living area. While we were framing, we saved all the scrap lumber we could to use as bracing for the trusses, knowing we would be standing them alone. When we finished, the trusses were all in place and held together by a mass of bracing until we could get the plywood decking on top. From the floor, it was like looking up at the sky through pick-up-sticks.

The next morning I reported for work as usual. Scott had to go to the lumber yard for some material. I walked through the opening that would one day be the front door heading for the utility room where we kept our tools at night. I got half way across the living room and stopped dead in my tracks.

I can remember asking myself, "What in the world do you think you are doing?" I was completely overwhelmed with the whole project. I thought to myself, "You can't build this house. Why are you spending all this money on this fly-by-night scheme anyway? No one in their right mind is going to come to Caney, Oklahoma for a retreat. What's wrong with you, are you crazy?"

I stood there for a long time, seriously doubting whether or not Scott and I could build this big house. But, the real question was whether or not I should be spending Jack's hard earned money on it. "What in the world was I doing?"

I remember thinking, I could strike a match to the whole thing right now, and I wouldn't be out that much money. That's what I should do; turn back now, before I wasted any more money.

Judges 7:3 *"...Anyone who trembles with fear may turn back and leave..."*

Turning Back

To turn back and quit was a song I had never sung in my life, but I was singing it that morning. As I stood there, I was convinced I would not be able to build the house. I was positive I shouldn't be spending the money on such a foolish idea. That was it, I would turn back. I would quit.

Just then I heard Scott's truck pull up. When he came in the house, he immediately saw I hadn't done anything. Normally I would have the compressor running, the nail guns out, the ladders set up, and everything ready for us to begin working. Not that day. I was just standing there staring off through the studded walls. I didn't even turn around to greet him when he came in.

In shock he asked, "What's the matter with you, are you sick?"

I turned to face him and answered, "No Scott, I'm not sick, but I am totally overwhelmed with this whole project. I'm doubting whether or not you and I can build this house, and if I even should be building it."

He almost ran to my side and put his arm around my shoulder and said, "Now don't you worry. I'm not going to leave you on this project. I will see it through to the end. You and I can build this house."

Then he added, "And, if we need to hire someone to help us we will, and if we need to rent a lift truck or some equipment, we will."

I thought to myself, "Sure, and whose money are we going to spend to hire someone and rent equipment?"

My feelings only intensified, as he continued consoling me, trying to get me to change my mind. I wasn't buying a word of it.

This was a stupid, hair-brained idea to begin with, and I had spent enough money already.

My entire orchestra had come against me. The violins were screaming that I was a fool. The whole brass section was blaring defeat, and the drums of failure beat so loud in my head I couldn't think of anything else. I was nothing more than a pitiful, stupid, idiot that had just spent a lot of money on something that would never succeed. How could I be so foolish?

Ezekiel 13:3 "...*Woe to the foolish prophets who follow their own spirit...*"

Divine Encouragement

As I stood there with Scott's arm around my shoulder completely consumed in the sounds of failure and defeat, something caught my eye above my head. I looked up to see what it was. Down through the mass of lumber and trusses came a lofting feather. It was gently falling, slowly drifting back and forth right in front of my eyes until it landed on the floor at my feet. As soon as I saw it, I knew exactly what it was. As it passed my eyes, the spirit of doubt left me completely.

Scott let go of me and headed for the door. "Where are you going?" I asked.

"To my truck to get my gun, there's a bird in this house." he answered.

"Wait." I said as I picked up the feather which was perfect, without blemish. Then I added, "There is no bird Scott, not this time."

I shared with him about Jack's love for feathers, after which he said, "Well, I don't know about you, but I'm feeling kind of encouraged."

"I am too, and there is not a doubt in my mind now. You and I can build this house, and I'm doing the right thing." I replied.

Scott took the feather and suggested we stick it up on the job like Jack would do if he were there with us. I agreed, and the feather remained on the job from then on.

The Maestro immediately brought clarity to the whole incident. I had come under attack that morning by Satan. God counteracted it by sending me a sign of encouragement only I understood. Scott thought it was an opportunity to go hunting, but I knew better. God couldn't have chosen a better sign to send; a perfect feather without a bird in sight. The feather was too long to fit between the trusses and yet it made it, without being deflected by the mass of lumber that was there at the time. Unbelievable!

This project was God's purpose for my life that He had shared with me four years earlier while we sat together on the plane. He had been reminding me of it all this time, and He prepared and provided the perfect person to help me build it. He was not about to allow Satan to destroy His plan.

Boy did I change my tune! I was ready to stop the music and call it quits, but with God on our team, we couldn't fail. As my grandpa used to say, "Alright, let's make some music."

Romans 8:31 *"...If God is for us, who can be against us?"*

The feather of encouragement

Roots of Faith

S cott and I fired up our tools and went to work, and we didn't quit. We never had to hire anyone to help us and we didn't have to rent any equipment. Together, the three of us built that house; Scott, myself, and God. What a team!

The duet Scott and I played was now a trio. God played the lead, and Scott and I harmonized right along with Him like we had played together for years. The job went great, and by mid- March, 2008 it was finished.

This was the largest house Scott or I had ever built. We both played the tune of completion and accomplishment, knowing full well all the praise and glory belonged to God, the Master Carpenter and Maestro.

While we were under construction, the Maestro filled my head with decorating ideas and it was remarkable how all the ideas came together.

The facility would have to be named, so one evening while going through some of Jack's things I came across all his books and information on trees.

Having worked in the lumber and timber industry for 42 years, Jack had a love for trees, and he shared this love with me often. He considered trees to be one of God's greatest creations. There are so many different kinds of trees and they each have a specific purpose; fruit trees, evergreen trees, shade trees, etc.

Often we would drive through the mighty Redwoods where we would stop and walk out among the giants. He loved to sit on the ground and look up through the branches which revealed the sky hundreds of feet above.

Once, while in a Douglas Fir grove, he told me of a time when a single Douglas Fir tree would supply enough lumber to frame an entire house. He talked of not only the magnificence of the tree but of the root structure, below the surface of the ground, which was as large and deep as the tree itself. Due to Jack's love for trees, we had many pictures, books and other items depicting different types of trees.

The next Sunday the Maestro cued Pastor Tom to preach on the importance of having deep roots of faith. With that, an idea was born. The retreat facility would be a place where folks could come to relax and grow closer to God, thus deepening their roots of faith.

I would call it The Treehouse. Each bedroom suite would be named after a tree specie that is found in the Bible and the décor would depict that particular tree.

Everything about it was fitting together perfectly, and a part of Jack would be there as well. Jack had been a part of everything I had done since 1973, and although he wouldn't be there physically, a part of him would be in The Treehouse, a big part of him. It would be wonderful, and Jack would have loved it. A horseshoe shaped rustic log cabin, with a 1,250 square foot open living area which has a large round dining table on one end and a game table, piano and library on the other. In the center of the room, a huge floor to ceiling rock fireplace with comfortable leather furniture creating a sitting area around a large redwood burl coffee table. The wood interior would add to the rustic feel as would the stained concrete floors.

I had the whole thing pictured in my mind. My orchestra rejoiced with praise to God for His plan and purpose for my life.

1 Chronicles 28:12 *"He gave him the plans of all that the Spirit had put in his mind....."*

Donations?

The job was progressing very nicely, by now Scott and I worked together like a well oiled machine. God was daily filling my mind with ideas and I could visualize The Treehouse completed, furnished, and full of people.

I also had been thinking along the lines that perhaps The Treehouse could bring in some added income which I was desperately in need of. I was able to do all the work, so there would be no added cost for employees. In addition I also knew about food cost and preparation since I also worked in catering in California for 25 years. I came to the conclusion that if I had two groups a month, I could generate enough income to pay my monthly expenses. That would be wonderful. I could easily keep up with the housekeeping, food, yard work, swimming pool maintenance and still host two groups a month. I had a plan, and it would be no problem.

Now the question was: How much to charge? As I lay in bed one morning praying about the subject, God spoke to my spirit, "Don't charge them anything, just let them make donations."

I wasn't sure if I heard Him right, so I thought I would run the idea past Scott. At the time we were in the process of putting the 1 X 6 tongue and groove pine on the ceiling in the living room, which was not an easy chore. We were both standing on ladders about sixteen feet apart with our nail guns, working on the ceiling when I sprung it on him.

We had the next board in place and after nailing my end I said, "I don't think I'll charge people to come here. I will just let them make donations."

With that, Scott dropped his nail gun over the side of the ladder, pointed his finger at me, and while looking at me through piercing eyes I had never seen before, he said, "You are crazy, and I don't want to ever hear you say that again." He grabbed the air hose connected to his nail gun, reeled it back in, and "bam," he shot a nail in the board. That was that, I wasn't going to talk to him about that subject again.

Over the next week I spoke with several others on the subject and they all told me the same thing, "You better be careful about that. People might take advantage of you." Surely God wouldn't want that, I must have heard Him wrong.

Hebrews 4:7 *"...Today if you hear his voice, do not harden your hearts."*

Attacked Again

I had allocated a certain amount of money to build The Treehouse, and I was doing a good job of staying within the budget. Jack and I invested in a bank in 1991, and it paid a quarterly dividend. The money from that made up a good part of my construction budget.

In November 2007, I received a packet in the mail informing me that our bank would be merging with a larger bank. The packet included the prospectus, which is a large document describing all the details of the merger and I took great pains in reading every page. A lot of it was way over my head, but there in bold print near the front of the document, it clearly stated if the merger was completed prior to a certain date in January, the shareholders of our bank would NOT be receiving their fourth quarter dividend. This could be bad news.

I picked up the phone and called the president of our bank who was a very good friend of mine, and asked him if he thought this would be the case. He assured me it would be complete, so I shouldn't count on the dividend. I had already counted on it. That was the money that was scheduled to arrive by the end of January, and I had it allocated for the final phase of construction and furniture. I knew full well that the big money in any job is in the finish work, not to mention all the furniture and decorations.

What would I do now? It was clear I wasn't going to receive that money. I had not planned to take any money out of my investments, but I might have to. I must admit, I spent a few sleepless nights worrying about it. Satan had another grip on me, and like before it was over money.

He was trying to take control of my orchestra and conduct it in another song of defeat and failure. I wasn't playing the song he had me playing that day in August when he attacked me hard, but my tune had changed from the happy refrain, *"Thank you God, we're almost through,"* to the down trodden song, *"Oh no, now what will I do?"*

Job 17:11 *"My days have passed, my plans are shattered, and so are the desires of my heart."*

Work and Worry

The job continued, and I didn't say a word to anyone, including Scott, about my financial dilemma. I didn't want Scott to become discouraged so I tried to not let it show. Scott and I worked every day just as we had since June, and I did my best to trust God and have faith that somehow it would all work out. We were so close to completion and yet so far away.

Scott and I knew how to play the song of work. It came naturally to both of us. The hum of the compressor, squeal of the saws, tapping of Scott's finish hammer, and bam, bam, bam, of our nail guns added the needed percussion.

December brought the usual added expenses of property taxes, Christmas, higher utility bills, and my annual health insurance premium, just to name a few. Every day after work I went to the Post Office to pick up my mail only to find another bill. The situation was getting worse, and the worse it got, the more worried I got.

Jack would have known what to do. He could always come up with the money we needed. What would Jack have done? Where was Jack when I really needed him? If I had paid more attention to him then I would know what to do now. How am I going to finish this project?

Satan was marching full speed ahead, piling it on me from all directions. The storm was intensifying with every passing day, and I couldn't get it off my mind. I did pretty well during the work day. However, every night as I lay down to sleep it became a full size marching drum and bugle corps blaring in my head, parading right over me leaving me flat in the road.

By the middle of January I was a wreck, and my full orchestra was playing the same song over and over again every night: *"Work, work, work"* every day and, *"Worry, worry, worry, over money, money, money."*

Jeremiah 50:42 *"...They sound like the roaring sea as they ride on their horses; they come like men in battle formation to attack you..."*

Good News

S atan was doing his level best to take control of my orchestra, but the Maestro stood firm on the platform and held tight to the baton. He wasn't about to let Satan's song overpower His! In a rage He flipped the page on the score, raised his mighty arms, and with a wave of the baton, brought the change I so desperately needed.

The next day after work, as usual I went to the Post Office to pick up my mail. I was relieved there were no bills, just some junk mail and the year end report on my investment account. I went home and opened the report.

I knew the stock market had been doing well, but Jack had taught me not to watch it on a daily basis, or it could drive you crazy. To be honest, I had been working so hard, I hadn't paid that much attention to it. I took the report out of the envelope. To my surprise my portfolio had grown considerably in the last year, even though I had drawn out a small amount each month for living expenses.

I knew it wasn't a good idea to take money out of my investment portfolio if I could help it, because I needed all the growth I could get. I had nothing else to generate monthly income, and it would be a number of years before I could apply for Social Security.

God was good! This news brought hope to my situation, and I didn't know how much longer I could have survived the nightly torment of the marching band plowing over me. It was the relief I needed, and it came at the right time, bringing with it a sense of security. If I needed to, and I probably would, I could take some money out of my investments to finish The Treehouse.

The Maestro had silenced Satan's marching band, and that night for the first time in a long time, I easily drifted off to sleep to the sweet lullaby of peace and security only God himself can play.

Isaiah 16:3 *"Give us counsel, render a decision..."*

Tile or Granite?

The pressure was off, but I would still be very careful, pinching every penny I could. God was good, but I wasn't going to take advantage of His goodness or take Him for granted.

We were almost ready for cabinets when Scott mentioned I would have to make a decision about the countertops. I really wanted granite, but I knew it would be expensive. Scott could see I was cutting costs everywhere I could, so when I mentioned granite his eyes opened real wide, and he tipped his head in question. Then he said, "You know, I could put ceramic tile on the counters. It would be beautiful, and cheap."

I knew Scott was a very good tile setter and would do a wonderful job. I also knew it would be cheap, but I really wanted granite. I had no idea what the cost would be, but I wanted it. It had been a long time since I got a price on a granite countertop, and that was in California where everything was more expensive. I had justified it to myself; low maintenance, no grout to clean, it's indestructible, it would accept hot surfaces, etc. I knew all about it and I wanted it!

A friend told me of a person who did granite work and was not too expensive, so I called him and he came over to measure and give me a quote. When he drove up he had a slab of granite on his truck that was exactly what I had in mind. The color, the pattern, and everything about it was just what I wanted.

He came in, took some measurements and went out to his truck to put together a quote for me. While he was outside figuring the cost, again Scott said, "You know, I can put ceramic tile on those cabinets for a lot less money."

The man came back in and gave me a price. I figured it would be considerably less than a California price, but his price was one third what I was expecting it to be. I questioned him about it and also asked him about the piece of granite he had on his truck. He said the price was correct and he had enough of that particular stone in stock to do my job. He also told me he could install it the following Friday. It was looking more attractive all the time. Even though the cost was a third of what I was expecting, it was still four times more than what the ceramic tile would have been.

I had a decision to make, and I did. I hired the granite man. Scott, who was on his knees working on the stairs at the time, fell flat on his face in disbelief. All night my orchestra played every version of "buyer's remorse," known to man. I had made the decision, and now I had to live with it.

Isaiah 16:3 "Give us counsel, render a decision..."

How Much?

S cott and I worked feverishly to get the cabinets set and leveled in preparation for the granite to be installed that Friday. We were making progress when my cell phone rang; it was the granite man. He would have to put me off one week because the bad weather we had been having made it impossible to complete his current job. Instead of this Friday, he would be here the following Friday without fail. That was good. Scott and I wouldn't have to work late leveling the cabinets and getting them just right.

The following week, we had the cabinets finished and we went back to working on the stairs. Thursday afternoon when I went home from work I noticed I had a telephone message on my answer machine. It was my friend, the wife of the bank president in California. The message was to call her husband at the bank as soon as I got this message. I quickly dialed his direct line number and he answered.

He was in a hurry and couldn't spend too much time talking to me because he had to call all the shareholders. Then he told me something I couldn't believe. He said that he had negotiated a partial fourth quarter dividend for us. Questioning what he had just told me, I said, "What? I have the prospectus on my desk and it clearly states that we will NOT be receiving a fourth quarter dividend."

"I know what it says, but I have negotiated this outside the prospectus." He insisted.

Who was I to argue with him, so I asked, "How much is it?"

He told me the amount per share which was a very odd number. Then he added, "The checks have been cut and are in the mail. You will probably receive it today. If not, you will definitely have it tomorrow." With that our phone call ended.

I went in the office to calculate the total amount the dividend would be. I owned a very odd number of shares, and the dividend was a very odd amount as well. When I multiplied it out, I couldn't believe the answer. It was twenty cents more than the cost of the granite I would be paying for the next day.

The Maestro struck up the band and we all played the most joyous song of praise and gratitude ever written, and we played it all night!

Psalm 37:4 *"Delight yourself in the Lord, and He will give you the desires of your heart."*

Perfect Timing

The next day the granite man arrived right on schedule and went straight to work installing the countertops. Scott was still working on the stairs and couldn't hide his shock over me going with the granite.

Normally I never left the job during the day, but that day was going to be special. At 9:30 AM I told Scott I was going to the Post Office and would be right back. I knew the check would be there and I knew how much it would be, to the penny.

I arrived at the Post Office, and sure enough there was the envelope from the bank. I didn't even open it. I just got in my truck and drove back to work. With the envelope in hand, I walked in the door and straight to where Scott was working on the stairs. He looked up at me and I tossed the envelope to him and said, "Open it. God just paid for the granite."

"What?" He asked.

I repeated myself, "God just paid for the granite. Open the envelope."

Scott took out his pocket knife, and opened it. He looked at the check and then up at me in total shock. I explained to him what it was and how it came about. Then I rubbed it in a little by saying, "See, God wanted the granite too."

He shook his head, handed me the check, and we both had a good laugh, not to mention a huge boost in faith.

In case you have never been involved in a stock merger agreement, all negotiations are made prior to the prospectus being printed. I have never heard of a dividend, or anything else, being negotiated outside a prospectus. In addition, the amount of the dividend was a very odd number, including a fraction of a cent, and I owned an odd number of shares, including a fraction of a share. If the dividend had been one tenth of a cent less, it would not have been enough to pay for the granite, and if it had been one tenth of a cent more, it would have been several dollars too much. The dividend was exactly what it had to be, to come as close to the cost of the granite as it did.

The Maestro led us all in "Our God is an Awesome God." Because, He is!

Job 5:9 *"He performs wonders that cannot be fathomed, miracles that cannot be counted."*

Blessing of Preparation

In mid April 2008, I hosted the first retreat group at The Treehouse which consisted of about twenty ladies from Ward's Chapel. It was a wonderful success, and I think my orchestra could be heard for miles around as together we played a medley of songs giving praise to God for not only giving me this purpose, but also for providing everything that was needed to plan, build, operate, and maintain this retreat facility.

While the group was there, I shared with them some of the story as to how the Treehouse came about. They asked me many questions about various aspects of the whole process. How do you know how to do this? Where did you learn to do that? Etc, etc. Their questions went on and on.

As I was answering them, the Maestro pointed the baton at me and gave me a tremendous revelation that brought a song to my heart which I have been playing ever since. The title: **"The Blessing of Preparation."**

God has blessed me with everything and everyone I needed to fulfill His purpose for my life now and what is still to come. Throughout my life I've done many things, some of which I have shared with you on the previous pages of this book. I realize now every opportunity to learn, and to experience things, has been a part of my preparation. The Maestro has given the cue to so many musicians who have played a part in my life overture.

Some played long, complicated parts, while others were short vignettes. Nevertheless, they all played, and with a wave of the baton they came in exactly on cue. The Maestro had prepared each musician, and knew precisely when to cue their parts.

As the revelation unfolded within me that day, I was as amazed as the ladies I was speaking to. I had not yet put the whole thing together. God told me He had something for me to do and He had been preparing me. Even though I heard it loud and clear in my spirit, I didn't realize it myself until that morning when I vocalized it to my friends.

It all came together in my mind as I spoke. God had been preparing me for this my whole life. What a revelation! What a blessing! The blessing of preparation.

1 Chronicles 28:19 *"I have...the hand of the Lord upon me, and He gave me understanding in all the details of the plan."*

The Treehouse

Gifts and Experiences

W hen I think of all the tools God has prepared me with, even I stand amazed. He instilled in me the eagerness and willingness to learn something new. My motto: If someone else can do it, I can too; I just have to learn how. Consequently, I have learned a little about a lot of things over the years.

When the Maestro gave me the cue to build The Treehouse, He had totally prepared me for every aspect of the building process. From working at our lumber yard and with Jack on our own building projects, I learned about lumber products and various building materials. I learned to read and draw plans, as well as do a complete material take-off (itemized material list).

Since Jack and I designed and built four houses ourselves, I was familiar with the building process and order of construction. I also learned to operate a wide variety of power tools and nail guns. Building is something I have always really enjoyed and God blessed me with the need to be "hands on."

My versatile job description at our lumber yard included the accounting, which God prepared me for in high school when I took what seemed to be the easy courses. They were easy for me, and God knew I would need them later. This knowledge enabled me to do all the bookkeeping for our lumber yard, the ranch, and our personal affairs. Now, The Treehouse is added to the mix.

God has also given me the spiritual gift of hospitality, and I saw that gift in action as a child through my Aunt Alice. I love to entertain people in my home. My catering experience afforded me the knowledge I need to prepare and serve food to large groups. Over the years I have fed as many as 750 people at one time at our home. Preparing food for large crowds of people doesn't scare me, in fact, the more the merrier. My desire is to make people feel at home in my home.

At some point along the way, I picked up a little knowledge about decorating, and it is something I enjoy dabbling with. I learned to sew from watching my Aunt Lil, and I do my best to make something out of nothing, as I saw her do so many times.

I didn't tell you earlier, but I owned a fabric store at one point where I learned about different fabrics and materials. This lent to my ability to make the window coverings, bed skirts, and other decorations at The Treehouse.

For eight months in 1970 I temporarily filled in for a graphic artist on maternity leave at the nationwide insurance company I worked for. I knew nothing about graphic arts, but during that time I learned to design forms and brochures which we cut and pasted together. I put this knowledge to work, and with the modern technology of digital cameras and computers, I easily designed a brochure for The Treehouse.

Everything mentioned here is part of my preparation by God. All these people and opportunities have played a part in adding to my knowledge and ability, which has enabled me to design, build, and operate The Treehouse.

Each has been a musician cued by the Maestro at precisely the right time to play their part in my life overture. When the Maestro cued a new musician, I didn't sit back and enjoy their music, I did my best to learn to play along with them. I studied their instrument and the tune they were playing. In most cases I never played as well as they did, but I did my best to emulate their song and play along.

Esther 4:14 *"...And who know but that you have come to royal position for such a time as this?*

Accomplished Musicians

The Maestro blessed me beyond my wildest imagination with the most accomplished musicians who, upon a wave of the baton, have played their best, and taught me much. In addition, are those who have played a tremendous, strong song of support over the years.

Jack was a generous person and gave me many wonderful presents and gifts, but the greatest gift I received from him, was the gift of his family. Very large in number, they have never ceased to play their fabulous song of overflowing love and acceptance of the city girl Jack introduced to the family so many years ago. In addition to his immediate family, there are literally hundreds of cousins who have added a variety of songs of support, guidance, and love to my life. It's a family like none other and I have been truly blessed by them as they have allowed me to be a part of their unique and fun choir of voices.

The Maestro provided me with two wonderful church families, who have consistently prayed and supported me for many, many years. Both my Country Oaks church family in California, and my Ward's Chapel church family in Oklahoma have continuously played a beautiful medley of hymns and spiritual melodies that have never failed to boost my spirits as they lift me up in prayer. The love and friendship given me by this group of devoted believing musicians makes for an unending song of support and joy.

My wide circle of friends, who are such a blessing, also play an important part in my melody of support conducted by the Maestro. They each play their part flawlessly and to perfection, coming in right on cue as the score dictates. He orchestrated how I would meet each one, and individually gifted them all to play their individual part.

In 1962 the Maestro cued the perfect musician to join me in playing a lifelong duet of friendship that continues to this day. For more than forty-eight years we have sat side by side playing in perfect harmony. Through the storms of the drums and the sweet love songs of the strings, together we play. When the storm of life was too grave for me to play at all, she played to me and for me. A wonderful musician whose song remains true and loyal, my dearest friend whom I love with all my heart, my Karen.

Job 16:20 *"My intercessor is my friend, as my eyes pour out tears to God."*

My Karen

Trust and Obey

After the first retreat I was on cloud nine playing the sweet melody of gratitude, for not only everything He had given and provided for me, but for the revelation of the blessing of preparation.

The phone began to ring and people booked retreats. I don't know how these people found out about The Treehouse, but they did. Group after group, all summer, fall and winter, they came. It was a tremendous amount of work, but The Treehouse was providing that added income I needed. My orchestra played the beautiful melody of praise which blended in perfect harmony with my middle ground theme song of work I enjoyed playing so much.

The next spring I was speaking to a retreat group when the Maestro cued me with another revelation that far exceeded the revelation of the blessing of preparation. The title: **"Trust and Obey, I Will Make the Way."**

Here's the way the blessing unfolded. God gave me a purpose for my life and totally prepared me for it. I tarried until God woke me up in January, 2007, at 3:00 AM, and preached a sermon to me through a woman preacher who said, "If God has been telling you to do something, this is the year to do it." I drew the plans, went to work, and built The Treehouse that year. It was finished in the March of 2008, and people began coming in April. It provided the additional income I needed.

Six months later, in October, 2008 the stock market crashed and everyone lost at least 40% of their investments. I was no exception. All the money I spent to build The Treehouse had been invested in the stock market.

If I had not been obedient to God's call that morning at 3:00 AM when He put the pressure on me, I never would have built The Treehouse. He knew what was coming. He knew the stock market was going to crash.

This has been a tremendous personal lesson in obedience. I have not always been obedient to God's voice, but I am so grateful I was this time. He gently tapped me on the shoulder and whispered in my ear for four years. Finally, He shook my cage and woke me up and threw me out of bed. Satan attacked twice, but He sent a feather as a sign of encouragement the first time, and an increase in my investment account and a check to pay for the countertops the second. This was God's purpose for my life, and He was bound and determined that I obey and not turn back, and I praise Him for it!

As this revelation unfolded in my mind, and I shared it with the people at The Treehouse, the Maestro cued my orchestra in the most beautiful rendition of *"I Know Who Holds Tomorrow"* that has ever been heard. This is one of the songs sung by my nephew, Lance Kell, at Jack's funeral and memorial service, and has meant so much to me since then, but this revelation brought a whole new outlook on the lyrics. God really does know what tomorrow holds, and He knows what lies ahead. If we trust and obey, He will make the way.

1 John 3:20 *"...For God is greater than our hearts, and He knows everything."*

Divine Networking

A nd so they came; group after group. The only form of advertisement was the brochure I designed and had professionally
printed. I distributed the brochures in the community and to some
churches, but most of the groups were coming from far away. How
were they finding out about The Treehouse? They each had their
story of how they "just happened to pick up a brochure somewhere,"
or "just happened to be talking with someone who had heard of
it." I did very little to market or advertise it because I was too busy
cooking, cleaning, mowing the lawns, maintaining the swimming
pool, and everything else it took to keep up.

I have heard it said that "word of mouth" is the best form of
advertisement, but I take exception with that. A word from GOD'S
mouth is the best! He was networking The Treehouse and doing a
better job than any professional advertising firm could begin to do.
He has had people lined up, waiting to come.

I had to smile to myself as I recalled overhearing people whispering behind my back, "She is crazy, no one is going to come to
Caney, Oklahoma to a retreat." The fact is, God is able to make a
plan successful, even one that others consider ludicrous.

The people who come are the continuation of His intricate plan.
This became obvious to me as the phone continued to ring, emails
arrived in my email in-box every day, and people just showed up at
the door.

My calendar was booking up faster and faster, and farther in
advance. People were reserving dates three, four, even six months

ahead. Dates for Christmas dinner parties were snatched up in July and August. God had put the word out, and people were responding.

It seemed like He wanted me to do more, but there are only 24 hours in a day, and I could only do so much. I was mowing the lawns after dark by the headlights of the mower now, how could I do any more!

In my spirit I voiced a simple prayer, "Lord, if you want me to do more here, I am going to need some help."

Psalm 20:4 *"May He give you the desire of your heart and make all your plans succeed."*

Not For Profit

In January 2009, I received a letter from the County Tax Assessor informing me that my property taxes would be increasing considerably. I went to the Assessor's office to speak with her personally about it. I attend church with her, and she had been to The Treehouse for a retreat.

After reviewing my file, she confirmed that the letter was correct and my taxes would be going up the next year. The increase was mainly due to the new construction of The Treehouse. She then suggested I look into forming a "not-for profit" corporation, which would make The Treehouse exempt from property taxes.

I left her office and drove straight to my accountant to discuss it with her. She was in agreement, and added I could take it a step farther and apply to the IRS for a 501(c)3 designation, which would exempt The Treehouse from income tax as well. Then she qualified it by telling me that she would be happy to download the 501(c)3 application for me, but she didn't want any part of the process. She added these applications are complicated and the process takes a long, long time.

She told me of an attorney in town that could assist me in forming the Not-for-Profit Corporation, and I drove back to town to discuss it with him. He was happy to help me and went right to work on the preparation of the Articles of Incorporation and the By-laws which are required by the State of Oklahoma.

When I asked him about assisting me with the 501(c)3 application to the IRS, he told me the same thing my accountant did: He didn't want any part of it. The process takes far too long and they continually need more and more information.

Within a couple of weeks The Treehouse was registered with the State of Oklahoma as a Not-for-Profit Corporation and that process was complete. I immediately took the needed documents to the Tax Assessor's office which she added to my file, exempting The Treehouse from property taxes.

The Maestro conducted my orchestra like a jazz band in full swing, all the way home. With their horns pointed high to the heavens, the whole brass section was swaying back and forth in time to their own music. Another huge blessing!

Deuteronomy 28:8 *"The Lord will send a blessing on your barns and on everything you put your hand to..."*

In Record Time

As I left the assessor's office I called my accountant and asked her if she would go ahead and download the 501(c)3 application from the IRS, and I would pick it up on my way home. What the heck, I could at least look at it and see just how complicated it was.

She had it ready when I got there and handed it to me in a LARGE envelope. Upon arriving home, I opened the envelope and took out the application. She was not kidding, it was thick and complicated, but I decided I would tackle it one question at a time and eventually I might get it completed.

I worked on it every day as time allowed. Finally, on the first day of June, I had it done. My accountant suggested I make a copy of it for my records and send it certified mail so I would know who signed to receive it. That was good advice, and that's exactly what I did.

The next day, June 2, 2009, I mailed the application off to the Internal Revenue Service in Kentucky. I was prepared for the long process which was ahead. I didn't have anything to lose. The worse thing that could happen would be for the IRS to deny my application and I would lose the $750.00 application fee.

Just as my accountant predicted, three weeks later I received a letter from the IRS stating they were in receipt of my application and they would be contacting me if they needed further information. I filed the letter and went back to work.

In August, I received a phone call from a woman who identified herself as the employee of the IRS who had been assigned to my case. She asked if I had a FAX machine as she needed more information. Since I had a FAX machine, she faxed me a single page document with three questions on it which I promptly answered and faxed back to her.

I heard not another word until October 18, 2009 when I went to the Post Office to pick up my mail, and there was a letter from the IRS. Assuming it was another request for more information I took it home. Upon opening it, I couldn't believe what I was reading: "Congratulations, your application for a 501(c)3 designation has been approved." I picked up the phone and called my accountant who asked me to bring the letter to her office. She wanted to see it for herself. I must be reading in incorrectly. She was as amazed as I was, my application had been approved in record time; less than four months. What a blessing!

Once again the Maestro struck up my brass section and conducted another jazz version of the song, "How Great Is Our God."

Genesis 49:26 *"Your Father's blessings are greater than...the bounty of the age-old hills..."*

My Way

One evening as I was sharing this blessing with a group of retreaters, the Maestro revealed to me the rest of the story, which would be the next revelation.

Being a Not-for-Profit Corporation and having a 501(c)3 IRS designation does not come without restrictions and criteria. To maintain a 501(c)3 status, a very large part of your income MUST come from contributions and donations. This meant I could no longer charge people to come to The Treehouse. I would have to depend on their contributions and donations to cover my expenses. Since everything I do, and provide for guests is totally free, they are able to deduct 100% of their contribution from their income taxes.

I would have to have faith and believe people would make adequate donations. However, I would never want to have someone not be able to attend a retreat due to financial reasons, so I felt very good about the whole situation. God had provided everything I needed to this point, and I had no doubt He would provide the income as well.

At that point in my testimony of God's goodness, the revelation hit me like a ton of bricks. I was transformed back to the day Scott and I were standing on the ladders putting up the wood on the ceiling in the living area. God had clearly told me not to charge people to come to The Treehouse, but to let them make donations. When I mentioned it to Scott, he dropped his nail gun, pointed his finger at me, and called my crazy. All the other people I discussed it with told me to be careful, that people would take advantage of me, which led me to believe that perhaps I had heard God wrong.

I had not heard Him wrong. He told me to not charge people, but allow them to make donations. It was obvious to everyone God had a hand in the approval of my 501(c)3 application with the IRS, which states that I CANNOT charge people to come to The Treehouse. It MUST be operated on contributions and donations.

It was as though the Maestro looked at me with a smirk on His face, and conducted my orchestra in Frank Sinatra's song, "I Did It My Way," with God changing the lyrics to, "You'll do it MY way." I'm happy to do it His way!

2 Samuel 22:31 *"As for God, His way is perfect..."*

Out To Dinner

In July 2009, I planned a road trip to the West Coast with my five year old grandson, Joseph. Knowing we would be back in the area I used to live, I called my good friend, Kelly Scharosch, and we planned for her to have a dinner party while I was there and invite some people with whom I used to attend church.

We used an old church directory to prepare the invitation list, and we came across a couple by the name of Arie and Mary Hoogeveen. I knew them slightly, but they were good friends of Kelly and her husband, Dennis. Knowing this, I suggested to Kelly that she invite them, to which she responded, "You don't even know them."

I said, "That's okay, you do. Invite them."

After discussing it back and forth a bit, she finally agreed to invite them, but didn't expect them to come.

Kelly and Dennis are wonderful party hosts, the party was a smashing success, and Arie and Mary were there. After dinner we were sitting around the dining table where I was sharing with the guests some stories about The Treehouse. Mary sat quietly at the end of the table, listening. I ended my remarks with an invitation to any of them who would like to come and visit. Dennis and Kelly had been to my place several times, and some of the others had been here as well.

As they were leaving, Arie said, "You never know, maybe we will see you in Oklahoma some day."

I was no sooner home and back to work when Kelly called to tell me that Mary really wanted to come with her to Oklahoma to see me and The Treehouse. My response was, "That would be great, make your plane reservations and bring her."

Kelly and Mary came for a ten day visit the end of August, and during that time we had a well known evangelist at The Treehouse as well as another group. In the ten days Mary was here, she was a tremendous help to me, and she caught the vision of ministry at The Treehouse. She also saw I could use some more help.

The Maestro had given Mary the cue to begin to play her melody of help in my orchestra and I saw how much easier it was to play my song of service and work with four hands instead of two.

Psalm 20:2 *"May He send you help...and grant you support..."*

New Musicians

W hen Mary got home she shared with Arie about the ministry at The Treehouse, and the fact that I needed help. Arie was a carpet installer and work was extremely slow, so they decided to come to Oklahoma for the month of November and help me.

I was thrilled and overwhelmed by their offer, and as Arie requested, I went to work making a list of things he could do while he was here. The list was not a short one, nor was it a list of easy tasks. It consisted of things I could do, but simply did not have the time. For example, stripping and resealing the entire outside of The Treehouse, pressure washing all the concrete at The Treehouse and around the swimming pool area, pouring concrete in front of my garage, cleaning out and fixing the leaks in all the rain gutters, and whatever else I could think of at the time.

I didn't know what to expect, but even if he did one thing on the list that would be one thing I wouldn't have to do. When they arrived, Arie went right to work. In two weeks time, he had every-thing on the list done, and done well!

While Arie worked outside, Mary and I were busy with one group after the other at The Treehouse. We quickly learned to work together as a team. It was great, and a lot was being accomplished.

In addition, by the time they left on December 2nd, we had The Treehouse completely decorated for Christmas and all the outside Christmas lights put up at my house. I was ready to start having Christmas brunches, lunches and dinner parties, and the schedule was full.

As Arie and Mary did not really know me, the fact that they even came to the dinner party at Dennis and Kelly's house is amazing. Also, the plane fares were reasonable and God worked out all the details which made it possible for them to come and stay for the whole month of November.

God heard my silent prayer for help and answered by preparing and sending Arie and Mary. When the Maestro gave them the cue to begin playing in my life overture, my part became a lot easier. Together we smoothly played a trio of service and accomplishment.

Psalm 66:19 *"...God has surely listened and heard my voice in prayer."*

Help Has Arrived

By the time they returned to California, Arie and Mary had made the decision that they would be coming back. In January, 2010 they packed some clothes and their little dog, and drove to Oklahoma with no return date in mind. They would just stay as long as they were needed and see how things went.

The phone rang constantly and my calendar was getting full with retreat groups coming just about every weekend. When spring arrived and the grass began to grow, Arie quickly learned to play the "mow, mow, mow the lawn" song, while Mary and I played "shopping and serving, brings cooking and cleaning."

When he wasn't mowing, Arie was washing windows, working in the flower beds, maintaining the swimming pool, and general outside upkeep. Arie likes to work outside and Mary enjoys getting to know the people, and as she says, "I love it all."

Week after week the groups came and our routine became seamless. With three of us working full time we could minister to more people at The Treehouse.

By early summer I was booking dates into the fall months and posed the question to Arie and Mary about their length of stay. I didn't want to get overbooked and not be able to keep up should they decide to return to California.

They prayed about it and decided they would go to California in August, sell most of their furniture, and prepare their home to be rented. I agreed to vacate a portion of my home so they could bring some of their own furniture and personal things. In September they returned with some furniture and personal belongings, and moved in.

Our work and ministry at The Treehouse continued through another busy Christmas season and into 2011, which brings me to the present. I don't know what God has in store for the future ministry at The Treehouse, I only know that I am ready, willing and able to play the familiar song, "Yes, Lord, Yes."

Psalm 90:17 *"...establish the work of our hands for us—yes, establish the work of our hands."*

Arie and Mary

Through It All

The Maestro has conducted my life overture through many passages and segments since the first down beat on October 21, 1950. Through it all He has stood firm and fast on the platform, presiding over the original score that God composed and orchestrated especially for me.

From the rumbling fierce storm of the timpani drum; to the sweetest love song ever played by a string section; the horror of the death march ending in total silence; brings the single tinggggggggg of hope from the triangle that overshadows a song of grief and tears. The true, pure tones of the woodwind's assuring song of purpose, to the crashing cymbals and off-key drone of Satan's attack; immediately followed by the soft blingggggggggg of the chimes, as a sign of encouragement sent drifting down from Heaven. The even, consistent tempo of the string section playing the rewarding song of service, harmonizes well with the ever present middle ground theme of work and accomplishment. Overridden by a mighty band of trumpets announcing the revelation of so many blessings!

From the original composition and orchestration, page by page, the Maestro has conducted my life overture. The number of pages left, and what is written there, is known only by the Maestro himself. Any musicians yet to be added are decisions that were made long before I was born, and He will give them the cue to begin playing at precisely the right time, just as He has done from the first measure.

My overture may end with the trumpets blaring and the final crash of the cymbals, or it may abruptly and unexpectedly stop. The score may dictate that it simply drift away with the lone fading note of the oboe, until it finally, completely disappears in the distance. Nevertheless, at some point it will end, and at that time I will step into eternity where there are no songs of sorrow or off-key melodies. No sadness or tears, or raging storms of drums. On that glorious day I will join voices with the angel band in the most beautiful, heavenly, everlasting song of praise ever written.

For now, I will continue to play my middle ground theme of work and service, in perfect harmony with my rejoicing song of praise and gratitude, to the King of Kings and Lord of Lords, Jesus Christ.

It is for Him I live, and Him I serve. It is for Him I have played my heart out and will continue to play until He, the Maestro, conducts the final beat, of the final measure, of the final passage of my life overture, just as He has conducted it all: With a wave of the baton.

Psalm 23:6 *"Surely goodness and love will follow me all the days of my life, and I will dwell in the house of the Lord forever."*

Back Stage

Back stage, the musicians reflect on the performance, each giving their critique and appraisal. They remember every missed cue, off-key note, and deviation from the score, but then are reminded how the Maestro pulled them back in rhythm bringing them into sync with the music.

Long before you were born, the Great Composer wrote a masterpiece: Your Life Overture. The Orchestrator has chosen and prepared the perfect musicians to play, and the Maestro knows the dynamics of every measure which has been designed to flow from one passage to the next. He never gives a miscue or makes a mistake.

All musicians do not play happy, joyous melodies in our life overtures. For some, their entire part consists of off-key, sour notes. Others appear to be out of rhythm or playing a tune that doesn't seem to fit at all. There are those whose song is wonderful music to our ears until all of a sudden, they go flat, or seem to get sidetracked, drifting off somewhere unrecognizable.

Nevertheless, in your life overture, every musician has been cued by the Maestro, and has played their part to perfection. Each musician, and every melody or rhythm they have played, is exactly what was written for you by the Great Composer.

Spend some time back stage with the Maestro reflecting on the musicians who have played thus far in your life overture. Identify your middle ground, or reoccurring theme song, which has appeared and reappeared throughout. Recall the different melodies, passages, interludes, and rhythm patterns. Study the many musicians who have played them and the movement of each passage.

As you visit with the Maestro, He will reveal to you the perfect work of the Composer and Orchestrator. These revelations will increase your faith and your certainty in knowing, that the Maestro is standing on the platform, at the podium. With the baton in His right hand, He is conducting the precise musicians to play their parts in every measure of your life overture. He does it all, with a wave of the baton.

Job 12:22 *"He reveals the deep things of darkness and brings deep shadows into the light."*

CPSIA information can be obtained at www.ICGtesting.com

228619LV00002B/118-999/P

9 781613 792520